UNESCO COLLECTION OF GREAT WORKS

ARABIC SERIES

"E. J. W. GIBB MEMORIAL" SERIES

NEW SERIES, XXI

AVERROES

ON THE HARMONY OF RELIGION AND PHILOSOPHY

A translation, with introduction and notes, of Ibn Rushd's *Kitāb faṣl al-maqāl,* with its appendix (*Ḍamīma*) and an extract from *Kitāb al-kashf 'an manāhij al-adilla*

by

GEORGE F. HOURANI

E. J. W. Gibb Memorial Trust

Published by
The E. J. W. Gibb Memorial Trust

First Printed 1961
Reprinted 1967, 1976, 2007, 2012 and 2015
Printed and bound by CPI Group (UK) Ltd, Croydon, CR0 4YY

ISBN 978-0-7189-0222-3

A CIP record of this book is available from the British Library

Further details of the E. J. W. Gibb Memorial Trust and its publications are available at the Trust's website

www.gibbtrust.org

PREFACE

I AM grateful to the International Commission for the Translation of Great Works and the Trustees of the Gibb Memorial Fund for sponsoring the publication of this book, and to the Graduate School of the University of Michigan for financial assistance towards research. I have been fortunate in having the translation carefully read and criticized by R. P. Georges Anawati, Professor N. Golb, Professor I. Kawar and Rev. Richard J. McCarthy; their help has led to many improvements and is warmly acknowledged. Very substantial, too, is my debt to the published works of Alonso, Asín, Bouyges, Gauthier, Goichon, Van den Bergh and others referred to in my notes. I thank my wife and Mrs. Cynthia Goldstein for typing the greater portion of my manuscript, and my wife for her encouraging interest which has sustained my effort.

GEORGE F. HOURANI.

Ann Arbor,
1960.

In memory of my father

CONTENTS

CONVENTIONS

The translation is based on the Arabic text in *Ibn Rushd* (*Averroes*): *Kitāb faṣl al-maqāl*, ed. G. F. Hourani (Leiden: E. J. Brill, 1959). But all references are to the *editio princeps* of M. J. Müller, *Philosophie und Theologie von Averroes* (Munich, 1859). The numbers in the margins of my edition and translation indicate Müller's pages and lines.

( ) Parentheses or numerations attributable to Ibn Rushd.

⟨ ⟩ Editor's conjectural additions to the text as found in the Arabic manuscripts.

[ ] Translator's explanatory additions, including all chapter headings and summaries.

The Arabic article is omitted in front of single names, e.g. "Fārābī" for "al-Fārābī", but "Abū Naṣr al-Fārābī". Diacritical marks are omitted where an Arabic name is incorporated in an English form, e.g. "Hanbalites", but "Ibn Ḥanbal".

INTRODUCTION

THE principal work translated in this volume is Ibn Rushd's treatise *Kitāb faṣl al-maqāl wa taqrīr mā bayn ash-sharīʿa wal-ḥikma min al-ittiṣāl*: literally "The book of the decision (or distinction) of the discourse, and a determination of what there is of connection between religion and philosophy".[1] Herein the author sets out to show that the Scriptural Law (*sharʿ*) of Islam does not altogether prohibit the study of philosophy by Muslims but, on the contrary, makes it a duty for a certain class of people, those with the capacity for "demonstrative" or scientific reasoning (*qiyās burhānī*). Apparent conflicts between the teachings of Scripture and philosophy can be reconciled by allegorical interpretations of Scripture, though such interpretations must not be taught to the common people. Such, in brief, is the message of *Faṣl al-maqāl*.[2] I have added the short appendix known as *Ḍamīma*, which illustrates further Ibn Rushd's doctrine on God's knowledge of particulars; and the last few pages of the related work *Kitāb al-kashf ʿan manāhij al-adilla* (to be referred to as *Manāhij*), because they contain an elaboration of his theory of interpretation.[3]

We know from the conclusion of *Manāhij* that that work was concluded in 575 A.H. (A.D. 1179/80). The date of *Faṣl al-maqāl* must therefore be set in the same year or one or two years earlier, since these works evidently form a series. What was the occasion which called forth such a work at this time from the philosopher of Córdoba? The treatise itself has the air of an answer to a challenge; and at one point Ibn Rushd writes: "If it were not for the publicity given to the matter and to these questions which we have discussed, we should not have permitted ourselves to write a word on the subject."[4] We have no record of the particular debate going on in Andalus at that time. We can, however, understand the occasion perfectly well in a more general way, in the light of the

[1] See Hourani (Arabic edition), note A, for justification of the Arabic title, and note 1 to the translation for further explanation of the title's meaning.

[2] See below, pp. 18-37, for a longer account of its contents.

[3] See Hourani, Introduction, p. vi, for the full titles of *Ḍamīma* and *Manāhij*. See note 189 to the translation, 25. 6-9, for explanation of the relation of *Faṣl al-maqāl* to *Manāhij*.

[4] *Faṣl*, 18. 16-18. All references to *Faṣl*, *Ḍamīma* and *Manāhij* are to the pages and lines of M. J. Müller's Arabic edition, *Philosophie und Theologie von Averroes* (Munich, 1859). These are given in the margins of my translation and edition.

historical background. This background may be divided into two aspects: the broad setting provided by the entire history of Islamic philosophy, and the special conditions prevailing in western Islam in the twelfth century A.D., including the personal history and situation of Ibn Rushd.

THE BACKGROUND IN ISLAMIC PHILOSOPHY

As soon as the study of Greek philosophy was introduced into Muslim circles, a certain tension between it and orthodox Islam was bound to exist.[1]

At the basis of Islam stood the *Qur'ān*, prescribing definite actions and beliefs to man. In the sphere of action, the weight of legal opinion in the first three centuries had decided that the right and the wrong for man were to be determined primarily by reference to the *Qur'ān*, supplemented by the Traditions; doubts about their interpretation were to be settled by the consensus of learned opinion (*ijmā'*); while independent reasoning (*qiyās*) by the lawyer was to be held as the last resort, and then only to be exercised in interpretation of Scripture, not in deducing the right or the wrong from the public interest, natural law, or any other standard independent of Scripture. Applying the same principles, early theologians set to work to formulate the system of doctrines about God and the world which was inherent in Scripture. The Mu'tazilites of the eighth, ninth and tenth centuries made some concessions to what seemed like principles of reason. For instance: the *Qur'ān* says that God punishes man after the Day of Judgement for his evil deeds in this life; but reason tells us that a perfect God would not punish a man for acts over which he had no control; therefore man must have power to choose his acts; therefore God does not predestine them. The opinion which generally prevailed, however, which was crystallized in the tenth century in the writings of Ash'arī and the Ash'arites, was that such concessions to principles of reason were not justified by any Scriptural authority. Thus, for example, the *Qur'ān* speaks of man as being responsible for his own acts; the *Qur'ān* also shows God as all-powerful and predestining man's acts; therefore both facts have to be accepted. The relation of man's responsibility to divine predestination was for the Ash'arites a matter of comparative detail, on which theologians might exert their ingenuity; but from the acceptance of both as facts they would not budge. Allegorical interpretation of Scripture might be used to explain certain statements, such as those which ascribe to

[1] See L. Gauthier, *La théorie d'Ibn Rochd (Averroès) sur les rapports de la religion et de la philosophie* (Paris, 1909), Introduction; A. J. Arberry, *Revelation and reason in Islam* (London, 1957); L. Gardet and M.-M. Anawati, *Introduction à la théologie musulmane* (Paris, 1948), pp. 318-24.

God bodily characteristics; but such interpretation was to be confined by the rules of Arabic philology concerning the normal speech of the Prophet's time.

This early development of Islamic theology proceeded without explicit reference to philosophy in the Greek tradition (*falsafa*). The relation of the Mu'tazilites to Greek philosophy is still somewhat obscure; they may have derived certain notions about God and man from it, or from Christian theology which drew upon it. Mu'tazilites and Ash'arites alike in their later period made use (without acknowledgment) of the weapons of Aristotelian logic in their debate. But neither party publicly referred to Greek philosophy as a source of true ideas about God and the world. Indeed the debate was half over before Greek philosophy became widely familiar to the learned world of Islam, in the middle of the ninth century. Thus *falsafa* appeared as something unnecessary, to say the least, to the working out of the theology of Islam.

But *falsafa* could appear positively dangerous to theology as worked out by the *mutakallimūn*. For it came with the pretensions of science, claiming to reveal demonstrative truth about the world with the same sureness as medicine, astronomy, mathematics and the other Greek sciences that came with it to the Muslim intellectuals of the ninth century. No thoughtful man could fail to be impressed by the depth of understanding and power of reasoning evident in the writings of the Greek philosophers, especially Plato and Aristotle. Their devoted followers the Muslim philosophers, such as Fārābī and, to a lesser extent, Ibn Sīnā, regarded them as sources of truth speaking with the authority of men who knew. On subjects of empirical science this mattered little to orthodox theology, because the Scriptures did not touch such subjects; but when the philosophers spoke of God, the world as a whole and the destiny of man, there was occasion for investigating whether what they taught agreed with what the *Qur'ān* and Traditions taught.

For two centuries, from the middle of the ninth to the middle of the eleventh century, a direct conflict between *falsafa* and *kalām* was delayed owing to a number of reasons. On one side, the Muslim philosophers had first to show their hands. This took time, the more so as they were conscious of working in an unfavourable climate and took pains to harmonize, as far as possible, the expression of their opinions with the basic doctrines of Islam. Thus Neoplatonic mysticism appeared in Fārābī and Ibn Sīnā as a species of Sufism; neither of them in their public writings directly denied the resurrection of the body; they offered a rational explanation for the rise of a Prophet; and so on.[1] On the other side, the Ash'arite

[1] See L. Strauss, *Persecution and the art of writing* (Glencoe, Illinois, 1952), ch. 1, for indications of Fārābī's caution in stating his opinions.

system of *kalām* did not become a dominant orthodoxy till after the establishment of the Great Seljūq Empire (after 1040), and especially after the foundation of the Niẓāmīya College in Baghdad (*c.* 1065) as a school of Sunnite theology. Before that, Shi'ite princes—Buwayhid, Fatimid, Hamdanid—had ruled Western Asia and Egypt, and had allowed more latitude for speculation to their subjects.

But around 1064, a warning note was sounded in Iran by Nāṣir-e Khosraw in his *Kitāb jāmi' al-ḥikmatayn.*[1] Nāṣir defends the rights of philosophic thought against the common enemies of philosophy and Ismā'īlī theosophy, the literalist doctrinaires whom he calls "*ahl-e-tafsīr*", "*ahl-e taqlīd*", "*ḥashwīyān-e omma*" and "*foqahā-ye dīn-e Islām*". They oppose "*ahl-e bāṭin o ta'wīl*".[2] They brand as a *kāfir* anyone who claims to know that objects have causal properties, e.g. that the sun will set because of its nature.

Nāṣir retorts that those doctors of religion are the real *kāfirs* because they ignore the injunction of the Prophet to reflect on the created world, though not on the Creator; thus they reduce Creator and created to the same level, and prefer ignorance to knowledge.[3] In moving words he laments the disastrous results of bigoted intolerance on science and philosophy.

> "Since those so-called scholars have denounced as infidels those who know the science of created things, the seekers after the how and why have become silent, and the expounders of this science have also remained mute, so that ignorance has overmastered all the people, especially the inhabitants of our land of Khorasan and the territories of the east."[4]
>
> "No one has written a book on the how and why of creation, because, out of the five causes which we have shown above to be necessary to the production of any book, first the seeker after this knowledge, who is the final cause, has ceased to exist, and secondly the expounder of this knowledge, who is the efficient cause, has also passed away; and with the disappearance of these two causes from among the people of this land, the science of religion itself has vanished. In the aforementioned land nobody now remains who is capable of uniting (*jam'*) the science of true religion, which is a product of the Holy Ghost, with the science of creation, which is an appendage of philosophy. For the philosopher relegates these so-called

[1] Ed. H. Corbin (Teheran-Paris, 1953), Introduction, pp. 60-64.

[2] *Ibid.*, Persian text, p. ١٠, §١٤.

[3] *Ibid.*, p. ١٠, §١٤; p. ١٢; p. ١٥. The Ash'arites denied causal connections between natural things, claiming that God is the only cause and that regularities in nature are due to His "habitual" regulation of it (*'āda, sunna*).

[4] *Ibid.*, p. ١٥, §١٩. As translated by A. J. Arberry, *Revelation and reason in Islam*, p. 72.

scholars to the rank of the beasts, and on account of their ignorance despises the religion of Islam; while these so-called scholars declare the philosopher to be an infidel. As a result, neither true religion nor philosophy remains any more in this land."[1]

But the most stunning blow to philosophy had not yet been delivered. This was Ghazālī's attack on it, made with full knowledge of its contents and all the force and clarity of his vigorous mind. This attack took more than one form. In his great *Tahāfut al-falāsifa*,[2] completed in 1095, he took a direct philosophic line and argued that the philosophers had not proved their un-Islamic theses of the eternity of the world, God's ignorance of particulars, and the impossibility of a bodily resurrection, besides other theses merely heretical. In *Kitāb fayṣal at-tafriqa bayn al-Islām waz-zandaqa*,[3] written between 1096 and 1106, he took up the legal question, what allegorical interpretations of Scripture were to be condemned as *kufr*, putting their holders beyond the pale of Islam; and he concluded that the philosophers' views on God's knowledge and the future life were to be so condemned. Finally, in his autobiography, *Kitāb al-munqidh min aḍ-ḍalāl*,[4] Ghazālī explained in a more personal and popular way how philosophy had failed to provide the cure that his own soul needed.

No one arose in the East to answer Ghazālī's challenge. Yet it had to be answered if philosophy was to stand a chance of survival in Muslim countries. It was this task which Ibn Rushd took upon himself, answering from the West some eighty years after the great Imām's attacks. There is little use in asking for an explanation of the eighty years' gap: the man for the occasion did not appear sooner, and might never have appeared. When he did, however, the challenge of Ghazālī was still felt to be a live issue; intellectual evolution was slower in those days. In Ibn Rushd's criticisms of Ghazālī we perceive a bantering animosity which treats "Abū Ḥāmid" almost as a living contemporary. *Tahāfut at-tahāfut* (*c.* 1180) is a point by point philosophic retort to the charges of *Tahāfut al-falāsifa*. *Faṣl al-maqāl* is to a large extent a legal retort to *Fayṣal at-tafriqa*.

The attempt of Ibn Rushd to harmonize two apparently different systems of thought was of a kind that had firm roots in Islamic culture. The *Qur'ān* itself in many places shows a syncretic tendency, in its teachings about the religion of Abraham and the rela-

[1] *Ibid.*, p. ١٦, §٢. As translated by Arberry, *op. cit.*, pp. 72-73.
[2] Ed. M. Bouyges (Beirut, 1927); also S. Dunyā (Cairo, 1947).
[3] In *Al-jawāhir al-ghawālī min rasā'il al-imām ḥujjat al-Islām al-Ghazālī*, ed. M. S. Kurdī (Cairo, 1934).
[4] Ed. J. Ṣalībā (Damascus, 1939); Eng. tr. W. M. Watt, *The faith and practice of al-Ghazālī* (London, 1953).

tion of Islam to Christianity and Judaism. The *Jam'* was a regular type of Arabic literature, which was well known in twelfth-century Andalus: Ibn al-Abbār's biographical dictionary mentions six books with titles beginning *Jam' bayna.*[1] In philosophy Fārābī's *Kitāb al-jam' bayna ra'yay al-ḥakīmayn Aflāṭūn al-ilāhī wa Arisṭūṭālīs* was an attempt to reconcile the philosophies of Plato and Aristotle, arising out of Fārābī's conviction that both sages had true knowledge of reality and therefore could not be in disagreement.[2] On the particular problem of the relations of religion and philosophy, four books from the eleventh and twelfth centuries are listed by Bayhaqī.[3] Nāṣir-e Khosraw's attempt to harmonize Ismā'īlī mysticism with *falsafa* has already been mentioned: it provides an interesting parallel, but it was almost certainly unknown to Ibn Rushd, having been composed in Persian for Shi'ite readers in Transoxania, on the north-eastern fringe of the Islamic world.[4] Ibn Ṭufayl's *Ḥayy Ibn Yaqẓān* briefly asserted the harmony of *shar'* and *falsafa*, though this was not its primary purpose.[5]

To all this background Ibn Rushd's treatise stands as a culmination, being the most direct and thorough *Jam'* of religion and philosophy that has survived from medieval Islam.

THE BACKGROUND IN WESTERN ISLAM

The local setting of *Faṣl al-maqāl* is the empire of the Almohades in the twelfth century. Here was an intellectual climate that was normally unfavourable to philosophy, but there were forces that for a short time encouraged it.

For several centuries before the twelfth, religious thought in Andalus and the Maghrib[6] was dominated by the Malikite system of Islamic law.[7] A network of casuistry (*furū'*, "branches"), covering every legal and moral situation, was elaborated on the basis of the work of Mālik Ibn Anas, the eighth century legal authority of Medina. The Malikite *fuqahā'* (lawyers) of Andalus and the

[1] *Kitāb at-takmila li kitāb aṣ-ṣila*, ed. F. Codera in *Bibliotheca Arabico-Hispana*, V-VI (Madrid, 1887-89). Index of books, VI, p. 900.

[2] Ed. F. Dieterici in *Die Philosophie der Araber*, XIV (Leiden, 1890). See especially pp. ١-٣.

[3] Ẓāhir ad-dīn al-Bayhaqī, *Ta'rīkh ḥukamā' al-Islām*, ed. M. Kurd 'Alī (Damascus, 1946). He mentions Ya'qūb Ibn Isḥāq al-Kindī (p. 41), Abū Zayd al-Balkhī (p. 42), Abū 'Alī 'Īsā (p. 75), Abū 'Īsā al-Munajjim (p. 110).

[4] See H. Corbin's Introduction to *Jāmi' al-ḥikmatayn.*

[5] L. Gauthier was mistaken in thinking it was. See G. F. Hourani, "The principal subject of Ibn Ṭufayl's *Ḥayy Ibn Yaqẓān*", *Journal of Near Eastern Studies*, 15 (1956), pp. 40-46.

[6] I use "Andalus" for Muslim Spain, and "the Maghrib" for Morocco, Algeria and Tunis.

[7] See M. Asín Palacios, *Ibn Masarra y su escuela*, 2nd ed. in his *Obras escogidas*, I (Madrid, 1946), for a survey of early Andalusian religion and philosophy, particularly of the ninth, tenth and eleventh centuries.

Maghrib felt no need for a system of theological dogma more explicit than that which was to be found in the Scriptures themselves. Their range of interests was summed up in the saying attributed to their master Mālik: "Knowledge is threefold: the clear Book of God, past Tradition (*Sunna*), and 'I know not'."[1] A certain number of Mu'tazilite thinkers appeared in Andalus in the ninth and tenth centuries, in spite of severe penalties imposed by the law on all views considered heresy (*bid'a*) or unbelief (*kufr*). The Ash'arite theology was familiar to Ibn Ḥazm of Córdoba in the eleventh century, though he claims that its influence had declined.[2]

In such a setting philosophy, with its un-Islamic inspiration, was even less likely to flourish. It is true that when the Greek medicine reached Andalus in the ninth century, its adepts could hardly help knowing something of its normal companion, Greek philosophy; but no record of this knowledge remains because they had to be discreet in mentioning it.[3] Ibn Masarra (883-931) was the first Andalusian philosopher, introducing a pseudo-Empedoclean pantheism, but he and his disciples only survived by living as hermits in the wilds of the Sierra de Córdoba; and at one point Ibn Masarra chose to go on a pilgrimage to Mecca rather than face legal charges of heresy at Córdoba.[4] After his death, philosophic studies were continued and persecuted alternately, according to the attitude of kings and the political conditions of each period; but nothing of distinction was created in these uncertain circumstances.

When the founder of the Almoravid dynasty in North Africa, Yūsuf Ibn Tashfīn, deposed the petty princes of Andalus after 1090, his action received the legal sanction of Ghazālī, among other doctors of East and West.[5] But this did not induce the Almoravides to show any favour to theology in their domains. On the contrary, 'Alī Ibn Yūsuf during his long reign, 500-37 (1106/7-1142/3) adopted a policy of honouring the *fuqahā'* and encouraging the study of Malikite law exclusively, and banning theology. A passage in the "History of the Maghrib" by the thirteenth-century historian, Marrākushī, describes the intellectual conditions in the reign of 'Alī Ibn Yūsuf:[6]

"No one had access to the Prince of the Muslims (*Amīr*

[1] Ḍabbī, *Bughyat al-multamis*, No. 861, ed. F. Codera and J. Ribera in *Bibliotheca Arabico-Hispana*, III (Madrid, 1885).

[2] *K. al-fiṣal fil-milal*, Span. tr. M. Asín Palacios in *Abenházam de Córdoba y su historia critica de las ideas religiosas*, V (Madrid, 1932), p. 102.

[3] M. Asín Palacios, *Ibn Masarra*, pp. 33-34.

[4] *Ibid.*, pp. 40 ff.

[5] Ibn Khaldūn, *K. al- 'ibar* in *Histoire des Berbères*, Fr. tr. M. de Slane, 2nd ed. P. Casanova (Paris, 1927), II, pp. 79-80.

[6] 'Abd al-Wāḥid al-Marrākushī, *K. al-mu'jib fī talkhīṣ akhbār al-Maghrib*, ed. R. Dozy, 2nd ed. (Leiden, 1885), p. 123.

> *al-Muslimīn*) or found favour with him except those who knew the science of legal deductions (*furū'*) according to the Malikite school. At that time the books of this school were readily bought and practice followed their rules. All other books were increasingly put aside, to such an extent that the study of the Book of God and the Traditions of the Prophet, peace on him, was forgotten, and not one of the famous men of that time concerned himself wholeheartedly with them. The people of that time went so far as to condemn as an unbeliever (*kāfir*) anyone who appeared to be entering upon the sciences of theology (*'ulūm al-kalām*); the lawyers surrounding the Prince of the Believers determined to proclaim the vileness of theology and the hatred of the early Muslims for it and their avoidance of anyone who appeared tainted with it; they proclaimed it a heretical innovation (*bid'a*) in religion, which often led to disturbance of the beliefs of its devotees, and so on. As a result a hatred of theology and theologians became firmly rooted in the Prince's mind, and he used to issue continual orders about it in the realm, insisting on the abandonment of any study of it and threatening anyone found in possession of literature on it. When the works of Abū Ḥāmid al-Ghazālī, may God have mercy on him, entered the Maghrib, the Prince of the Muslims ordered them to be burnt, and issued severe threats of execution and confiscation of property against anyone found in possession of any of them; and these orders were strictly enforced."

When the reformer Ibn Tūmart started expounding Ash'arite theology at Fez, he was expelled at the prompting of the lawyers, who urged that his teaching might corrupt the masses.[1]

It might be expected that in such an environment philosophy would fare even worse than theology; but in fact the opposite was the case, and philosophy enjoyed a quiet revival. On one hand an order of Ṣūfīs flourished at Almeria, whose doctrines Asín thought must have been in the direct line of transmission between Ibn Masarra and Ibn 'Arabī, and thus Neoplatonic and pantheistic in character.[2] On the other hand the first Andalusian philosopher to make direct use of the works of Plato and Aristotle appeared in this period, Ibn Bājja (Avempace). Later philosophers agreed in considering Ibn Bājja the first philosopher of merit in Andalus;[3]

[1] *K. al-mu'jib fī talkhīṣ akhbār al-Maghrib*, p. 132.

[2] M. Asín Palacios, *Ibn Masarra*, pp. 142 ff. Asín admitted that there was no direct documentation on the beliefs of the Almeria Ṣūfīs, but argued from resemblances of doctrine at the two ends and chains of disciples in between.

[3] Ibn Ṭufayl, *Ḥayy Ibn Yaqẓān*, 2nd ed. L. Gauthier (Beirut, 1936), pp. ١٢-١٣; Ben Maymōn (Maimonides). *Guide for the perplexed*, Part 2, ch. 9: Eng. tr. M. Friedländer, 2nd ed. (London, 1904); Ibn Abī Uṣaybi'a, *'Uyūn al-anbā' fī ṭabaqāt al-aṭibbā'*, ed. A. Müller (Königsberg, 1884), II, pp. 62-64.

perhaps they ignored Ibn Masarra because they did not consider him a true *faylasūf* in the tradition of Plato and Aristotle. Another philosopher, Ibn Ṭufayl, passed most of his life under the Almoravid dynasty, though his surviving philosophic work, *Ḥayy Ibn Yaqẓān*, belongs to the Almohad period. Moreover, there must have been some good teachers of philosophy at Córdoba, for the distinguished philosophers of the next generation, Ibn Rushd and Mōshe Ben Maymōn (Maimonides), received their education there in the last years of the Almoravides.[1]

Thus it is clear that there was a lively interest in philosophy in Andalus under the Almoravides. Why it grew up in this period is somewhat of a puzzle. A negative reason may be suggested: that whereas the Almoravides and their supporters, the lawyers, feared Ash'arite preaching to the people, they had no such fear of philosophers because of the philosophers' strong tradition of discretion and their strict and deliberate limitation of their audience.[2]

Yet philosophy remained under its usual cloud of suspicion. A contemporary of Ibn Bājja, Ibn Wahīb, ceased to speak openly of philosophy, owing to the dangers to life; he devoted his later life to writing books on the Islamic sciences: "neither was there found in them, as in the works of others, anything hidden to be explained after his death".[3] In Ibn Bājja's *Kitāb tadbīr al-mutawaḥḥid* there is a sense of loneliness: the philosophers are called "weeds" (*nawābit*), like the grass that springs up among the crops; they are strangers in their own country, one of an exceedingly small number. A philosopher may even find no kindred spirit in his country, in which case he will have to live in solitude or emigrate.[4]

A new stage in the intellectual history of western Islam was reached when Ibn Tūmart, the Mahdī of the Almohades (probably d. 622 = 1128), introduced eastern theology (*kalām*) among his disciples. On some questions, such as the denial of the divine attributes, he adopted a Mu'tazilite position; on others, such as allegorical interpretation (*ta'wīl*) of the anthropomorphic passages of Scripture, he followed the Ash'arites. In law he was a Zahirite: that is to say, he believed in taking the Scriptures in their literal sense and judging their meaning directly, following no legal

[1] Ibn Rushd was born in 520 (1126/7), Ben Maymōn in 530 (1135). Seville was captured by the Almohades in 541 (Jan., 1147), Córdoba was surrendered to them in 543 (1148/9). Ibn Bājja died young, in 533 (1138/9), and could not have been the teacher of Ibn Rushd or Ben Maymōn. Nor did he ever meet Ibn Ṭufayl (*Ḥayy Ibn Yaqẓān*, p. ١٣).

[2] See *Faṣl*, *passim*, and notes 142, 191 to the translation; I. Goldziher, Introduction to *Le livre de Mohammed Ibn Toumert, mahdi des Almohades*, ed. J. D. Luciani (Algiers, 1903), pp. 74-79.

[3] Ibn Abī Uṣaybi'a, *'Uyūn al-anbā'*, II, p. 63.

[4] Ed. and Span. tr. M. Asín Palacios, *El regimen del solitario por Avempace* (Madrid-Granada, 1946), pp. ١٠-١١, ٧٨-٧٩.

authority such as Mālik but only the general principles of jurisprudence (*uṣūl al-fiqh*). He began a programme of popular religious education in North Africa, preaching and writing in Berber, formulating a short creed, and compiling collections of Traditions on prayer, purification, booty and wine. All this was in opposition to the traditional attitude of the educated classes in the West, described in the preceding pages. Thus in some respects the Mahdī's movement had the character of a protestant reformation: it was a movement aiming to bring Scripture and people closer to each other.[1]

The opposition of the Almoravides to such a programme was inevitable. In the armed conflict between the two Berber groups, the Almohades overthrew the kingdom of the Almoravides in North Africa by 541 (1146/7) and in the next few years conquered their Andalusian provinces. The conqueror, 'Abd al-Mu'min (r. 527-58 = 1132/3-1163), was the designated successor of the Mahdī, and it must have been in his reign that the books of the Ash'arite theologians and Ghazālī first became widely familiar to the educated public of the West.[2] In law, as befitted the Mahdī's successor, he was a convinced Zahirite (literalist) and opponent of the *furū'* (positive law), but he kept these opinions to himself,[3] because the class of Malikite lawyers was strongly entrenched in his new empire and must provide a large part of the personnel of his civil administration.

'Abd al-Mu'min's interests, however, were not limited to the Islamic sciences. The scholars whom he gathered round him and encouraged were divided into two classes of "students" (*ṭalaba*): the learned traditionists of the original Almohad movement (*ṭalabat al-Muwaḥḥidīn*), who were of the Maṣmūda tribe, and the city scholars (*ṭalabat al-ḥaḍar*) on every science. The leaders of these two groups attended his Councils of State, both public and closed, and the sessions always began with discussion of a learned question, stated by the Prince himself.[4] Thus the puritanical movement of Ibn Tūmart was being broadened somewhat (at any rate within

[1] See I. Goldziher, Introduction to *Ibn Toumert*, and "Materielien zur Kenntniss der Almohadenbewegung", *Zeitschrift der Deutschen Morgenländischen Gesellschaft*, **41** (1887), pp. 30-140; R. Brunschvig, "Sur le doctrine du Mahdi Ibn Tūmart", *Arabica*, **2** (1955), pp. 137-49. For recently discovered sources on the history of these times see especially E. Lévi-Provencal, Introduction to *Documents inédits d'histoire Almohade* (Paris, 1928), and "'Abd al-Mu'min", *Encyclopaedia of Islam*, 2nd ed. (Leiden, 1954-).

[2] See below, p. 16, on knowledge of Ash'arite and Ghazalian writings in Andalus in the 1170s.

[3] Marrākushī, *Mu'jib*, p. 203. Such a statement, about the concealed opinions of someone who died 60 years before the date of writing, might be suspected; but it has circumstantial probability in both parts.

[4] Marrākushī, *Mu'jib*, pp. 144, 249. See J. F. P. Hopkins, "The Almohade hierarchy", *Bulletin of the School of Oriental and African Studies*, **16** (1954), pp. 93-112.

the limits of Islam, for this was the time of the forced conversions of Spanish Christians and Jews). This development was to continue on the basis of the good education given by 'Abd al-Mu'min to his sons.[1]

The intellectual tendencies of 'Abd al-Mu'min are found intensified in his son and successor Abū Ya'qūb Yūsuf (r. 558-80 = 1163-84). The cast of mind of this remarkable man, whom Marrākushī calls the only true king of the Almohades,[2] had far-reaching consequences in the history of thought, for it gave a new boost to philosophy in Islam at a time when it could bear fruit in Jewish and Christian circles, in Spain and the rest of Europe. For this reason, and because of their direct bearing on *Faṣl al-maqāl*, I shall devote some attention to Abū Ya'qūb's scholarly interests and activities.

The education which he had received from his father was augmented by himself when he was a provincial governor at Seville, after 551 (1156/7), for he took the opportunity to learn from the scholars there in every subject.[3] In law he was a cautious Zahirite and opponent of the *furū'*, like his father, but he ventured beyond him in revealing this attitude: thus, in the course of a meeting with a certain scholar, he is said to have rejected the varying interpretations of the lawyers and declared that the only authorities acceptable to him were the Scriptures and the sword.[4] He was an extremely learned traditionist, thoroughly familiar with the *Qur'ān* and Traditions;[5] he compiled a book of Traditions on holy war (*jihād*), in continuation of the series of such compilations initiated by Ibn Tūmart.[6]

There is no doubt that Abū Ya'qūb had a passion for learning, and above all for philosophy. Like his father, he used to begin his Councils with discussion of a learned question with the two classes of scholars.[7] Marrākushī writes that he

> "continued to collect books from Andalus and the Maghrib, and to seek out men of learning, especially theoretical scientists (*ahl 'ilm an-naẓar*),[8] until he had gathered round him more

[1] Ibn Khallikān, *Wafayāt al-a'yān* (Cairo, 1859), II, p. 491, = Eng. tr. M. de Slane, IV (Paris, 1871), p. 471.

[2] Marrākushī, *Mu'jib*, p. 176.

[3] *Ibid.*, p. 170; Ibn Khaldūn, *Histoire des Berbères*, II, p. 192, gives the date.

[4] Marrākushī, *Mu'jib*, p. 203.

[5] *Ibid.*, p. 170; I. Goldziher, *Z.D.M.G.*, 41 (1887), p. 98, with reference to Ibn Ṣāḥib aṣ-Ṣalāt, Oxford Marshall MS. 433, fol. 45a; *ibid.*, pp. 134-38, the text of a decree to his provincial judges which shows his competence and traditionalism in law.

[6] Marrākushī, *Mu'jib*, p. 183; I. Goldziher, *Z.D.M.G.*, 41 (1887), pp. 81, 99.

[7] Marrākushī, *Mu'jib*, p. 249.

[8] This term includes philosophers. Cf. Ibn Khallikān, *Wafayāt* (Cairo, 1859), II, p. 491, = Eng. tr. M. de Slane, IV, p. 471: Abū Ya'qūb preferred philosophy to literature and other subjects.

> than any previous king of the Maghrib. One of the versatile men of learning who accompanied him was Abū Bakr Muḥammad Ibn Ṭufayl, one of the Muslim philosophers who had mastered all the parts of philosophy. The Prince of the Believers (*Amīr al-Mu'minīn*) Abū Ya'qūb was extremely attached and devoted to him: I have heard that he used to stay in the Prince's palace with him for days, without emerging for nights and days on end."[1]

Ibn Ṭufayl was in fact chief physician to the monarch, but it could not have been medicine which held them so long in converse; it must have been philosophy and religion. Ibn Ṭufayl was now in his later years, and much interested in religion; among other things he was anxious to reconcile philosophy with religion (*al-jam' bayn al-ḥikma wash-sharī'a*).[2]

It was Ibn Ṭufayl who both introduced Ibn Rushd to Abū Ya'qūb and commissioned him to execute the Prince's wish that commentaries should be written on the works of Aristotle. The two events are narrated in succession by Marrākushī, and should probably both be dated between 563 and 564 (1168-69).[3] The narrative of Marrākushī is based on accounts given by Ibn Rushd himself to one of his pupils, and is of such interest and significance for our subject that I reproduce it in full:

> "This Abū Bakr [Ibn Ṭufayl] continued to draw men of learning to the Prince from every country, bringing them to his attention and inciting him to honour and praise them. It was he who brought to the Prince's attention Abul-Walīd Muḥammad Ibn Aḥmad Ibn Muḥammad Ibn Rushd; and from this time he became known and his ability became celebrated among men. Ibn Rushd's pupil, the lawyer and professor Abū Bakr Bundūd Ibn Yaḥyā al-Qurṭubī told me that he had heard the philosopher Abul-Walīd say on more than one occasion:
>
> "'When I entered into the presence of the Prince of the Believers, Abū Ya'qūb, I found him with Abū Bakr Ibn Ṭufayl alone. Abū Bakr began praising me, mentioning my family and ancestors and generously including in the recital things beyond my real merits. The first thing that the Prince of the Believers said to me, after asking me my name, my father's name and my genealogy was: "What is their opinion about the heavens?"—referring to the philosophers—"Are they eternal or created?" Confusion and fear took hold of me,

[1] *Mu'jib*, p. 172.
[2] *Ibid.*, p. 172; Ibn Khallikān, *Wafayāt*, II, p. 493, = Eng. tr. de Slane, IV, p. 474.
[3] See L. Gauthier, *Ibn Thofaïl, sa vie, ses oeuvres* (Paris, 1909), pp. 15-17.

and I began making excuses and denying that I had ever concerned myself with philosophic learning; for I did not know what Ibn Ṭufayl had told him on the subject. But the Prince of the Believers understood my fear and confusion, and turning to Ibn Ṭufayl began talking about the question of which he had asked me, mentioning what Aristotle, Plato and all the philosophers had said, and bringing in besides the objections of the Muslim thinkers against them; and I perceived in him such a copious memory as I did not think could be found [even] in any one of those who concerned themselves full time with this subject. Thus he continued to set me at ease until I spoke, and he learned what was my competence in that subject; and when I withdrew he ordered for me a donation in money, a magnificent robe of honour and a steed.'

"That same pupil of his also told me that Ibn Rushd had told him:

"'Abū Bakr Ibn Ṭufayl summoned me one day and told me, "Today I heard the Prince of the Believers complain of the difficulty of expression of Aristotle and his translators, and mention the obscurity of his aims, saying, 'If someone would tackle these books, summarize them (*yulakhkhiṣuhā*)[1] and expound their aims, after understanding them thoroughly, it would be easier for people to grasp them.' So if you have in you abundant strength for the task, perform it. I expect you will be equal to it, from what I know of the excellence of your mind, the purity of your nature, and the intensity of your application to science. I myself am only prevented from this undertaking by my age, as you see, my occupation with government service, and the devotion of my attention to matters which I hold more important."'[2] Abul-Walīd said: "This was what led me to summarize (*talkhīṣ*) the books of the philosopher Aristotle." ' "[3]

There are several points in this account that call for our special attention. It is clear that Abū Ya'qūb was highly interested and learned in philosophy, and that it was he who took the initiative in instituting the great project of Arabic commentaries on Aristotle which Ibn Rushd carried out. Even more significant for our subject, however, is the fact that until the interview with the

[1] On the meaning of *talkhīṣ* see below, p. 15, n. 5.

[2] I believe there could only have been one thing which a Muslim philosopher talking to another would refer to as more important than government service: the care of his own soul. That this is what Ibn Ṭufayl means here is confirmed by the subject and spirit of his book *Ḥayy Ibn Yaqẓān*, and by the statement of Marrākushī, *Mu'jib*, p. 172, that "at the end of his life he turned his attention to metaphysics (*al-'ilm al-ilāhī*) and put aside other studies".

[3] *Mu'jib*, pp. 174-75.

Prince Ibn Rushd was unaware of his favourable interest in philosophy, and feared some harsh penalty if he himself were known to be occupied in such a study. Nothing could more plainly illuminate the public unpopularity of philosophy than the Prince's extreme discretion and the philosopher's apprehensions.

It is time now to consider, to an extent that may enlighten our subject, who this man was who received the confidence of the Prince and his philosophic physician. Ibn Rushd came from a distinguished Cordoban family of lawyers. His grandfather, Abul-Walīd the elder (450-520 = 1058/9-1126/7), was a chief justice (*qāḍī al-jamā'a*) in Córdoba, who wrote two celebrated law books in the Malikite fashion.[1] Towards the end of his life he was active in appealing to the Almoravid 'Alī Ibn Yūsuf to act more decisively against the Christians in Andalus. Less is known about Ibn Rushd's father, but he too was a *qāḍī* at Córdoba.

There is little direct evidence about Ibn Rushd's early life, but it is clear that he grew up in one of the best homes in Córdoba during the later years of the Almoravid regime. In such a family it was natural that he should receive a good legal education. His law teachers are mentioned in the short biography of him by Ibn al-Abbār, who also states that Ibn Rushd memorized the *Muwaṭṭā* of Mālik.[2] At some time in his life he wrote three or four books on law;[3] Ibn al-Abbār praises them highly, as well as his opinions as a lawyer and decisions as a judge.[4]

Among the list of his studies in youth Ibn al-Abbār mentions theology (*'ilm al-kalām*).[5] His writings confirm his first-hand knowledge of Ash'arite works, such as those of Abul-Ma'ālī al-Juwaynī, known as Imām al-Ḥaramayn, the teacher of Ghazālī; and he was thoroughly familiar with the works of Ghazālī. Concerning the Mu'tazilites he confessed that their books had not reached Andalus,[6] but he had a general knowledge of their teachings. Thus it is evident that he was well versed in the traditional Islamic sciences of jurisprudence and theology; his later distaste for *kalām* was not due to ignorance, but to a strong conviction that it was muddled and not scientific as he thought philosophy was.

On the side of secular studies, he is said to have possessed a wide

[1] See C. A. Nallino, "Intorno al kitāb al-bayān del giurista Ibn Rushd", in *Homenaje á D. Francisco Codera* (Saragossa, 1904), pp. 67-77; Ibn Khaldūn, *Muqaddima*, in *Prolégomènes d'Ebn Khaldoun*, ed. E. M. Quatremère (Paris, 1858), III, p. 11.

[2] *Takmila*, in *Bibliotheca Arabico-Hispana*, V, pp. 269-70; also in E. Renan, *Averroès*, pp. 435-37.

[3] Ibn al-Abbār, *Takmila*, pp. 269-70; Ibn Abī Uṣaybi'a, *'Uyūn al-anbā'*, II, p. 77; also in E. Renan, *Averroès*, p. 453.

[4] *Takmila*, pp. 269-70.

[5] *Ibid.*, p. 269.

[6] *Manāhij*, 42.

knowledge of Arabic literature.[1] But it was towards the Greek sciences that he obviously showed the greatest enthusiasm. He was thoroughly educated in medicine, and wrote his "General medicine", *Al-Kullīyāt fiṭ-ṭibb*, in the earlier part of his career—not after 1169 at the latest.[2] It is evident from his writings that he was thoroughly familiar with the whole body of Aristotelian science.

We know hardly anything about his philosophic education. He could not have been a student of Ibn Bājja who died when Ibn Rushd was twelve, and it is unlikely that he ever studied under Ibn Ṭufayl.[3] One of his teachers in philosophy was a certain Abū Ja'far Hārūn, but nothing is known about this man's philosophic ideas, beyond the fact that he was a careful student of Aristotle and other ancient philosophers.[4] Very probably it was under him that Ibn Rushd first studied that Aristotelian philosophy which became the dominant intellectual passion of his life.

Before the interviews in Marrākush, Ibn Rushd's writings were on medicine (*the Kullīyāt*), on Aristotle (several of the summaries),[5] and, presumably, on law. Thus at the time of these interviews he appeared before the Almohad ruler and Ibn Ṭufayl as a man in his early forties, with a very broad education, who had already done important work in science and philosophy. We may add that he had a sharp analytical mind and a certain wit and lucidity in expression; these qualities are evident in his writings and in the few sayings of his which have been preserved by biographers and historians.

From the time of the interviews (1168/69), Ibn Rushd "became known and his ability became celebrated among men".[6] Assured of the ruler's backing, he worked for the next decade on his task, principally on the middle commentaries: first at Seville, then at

[1] Ibn al-Abbār, *Takmila*, p. 269.

[2] See L. Gauthier, *Ibn Rochd*, p. 12.

[3] *Ibid.*, pp. 4-5; and see below, p. 18.

[4] Ibn Abī Uṣaybi'a, *'Uyūn al-anbā'*, II, pp. 75 and 76.

[5] For the chronology of Ibn Rushd's philosophical works, see M. Alonso, *Teología de Averroes* (Madrid-Granada, 1947), pp. 51-98; L. Gauthier, *Ibn Rochd*, pp. 12-14. Alonso, pp. 55-68, gives good reasons for dating the summaries of Aristotle's Organon before 1159, and the first edition of the summaries of six other works in 1159. In view of these reasons I do not see the force of Gauthier's conclusion, p. 13, n. 1, that the latter group must be after 1169. Gauthier's view is based on the statement of Ibn Rushd, as reported by Marrākushī, *Mu'jib*, pp. 174-75, that it was the royal commission, probably given in 1169, that led him to make "ces paraphrases". The word used is *talkhīṣ*: but this word may be used here loosely, to refer to the middle commentaries not the summaries. On the complicated question of the meaning of *talkhīṣ*, see A. F. Ahwani, Introduction to Ibn Rushd's *Talkhīṣ kitāb an-nafs* (Cairo, 1950), pp. 9-18. A general consideration may be added: it seems improbable that Abū Ya'qūb and Ibn Ṭufayl would have commissioned for their important project a scholar who had not yet published any works on Aristotle.

[6] Marrākushī, *Mu'jib*, p. 174.

Córdoba to which he returned soon after 566 (1170/1).[1] He refers in his works to distractions and difficulties which prevented full attention to his studies. It is very probable that he was filling posts as a *qāḍī*, though I find no evidence of date for this before 577 (1181/2), when a late chronicle records that he was appointed *qāḍī* of Córdoba.[2] After some years of commenting, Ibn Rushd turned aside to write the three related treatises, *Faṣl*, *Ḍamīma* and *Manāhij*: the last was completed in 575 (1179/80). According to Alonso's chronology, they fall between the period of the middle commentaries and that of the great commentaries. He had completed his *Middle commentary on Aristotle's Ethica Nicomachea* in 572 (1176/7), and perhaps wrote his *Commentary on Plato's Republic* soon after that.[3]

We may now return to the question which remains to be answered concerning *Faṣl*: what was the local occasion for the writing of a defence of philosophy? In the absence of direct evidence of a particular challenge to philosophic activities in the 70's of the twelfth century, we have to infer the occasion from our knowledge of the total situation as described in the preceding pages. It is clear enough that, although the prince could secure the personal safety and well being of his protégé, he could not suppress vocal opposition to philosophy by all the forces that condemned it. These forces comprised the conservative Malikite lawyers and their popular supporters, and the rising class of Ash'arite theologians who had received the blessing of the Mahdī and who were "considered orthodox by most people today", according to Ibn Rushd's statement in *Manāhij*.[4] Nothing had occurred to abate the widespread and long-standing hostility to philosophy, of which ample evidence has been mentioned above. That it persisted in the later years of the twelfth century is shown by Abū Yūsuf's sharp persecution of philosophers (including Ibn Rushd) in 1195, evidently with the approval of a

[1] Summary of Aristotle's *Meteorologica* = *K. al-āthār al-'alawīya*, p. 53 in *Rasā'il Ibn Rushd* (Hyderabad, 1947): Ibn Rushd was not at Córdoba at the time of the first earthquake there in 566, but was present during the lesser tremors of the following two years.

[2] *Chronique des Almohades et des Hafsides*, Fr. tr. E. Fagnan (Constantine, 1895), p. 16: a sixteenth-century work attributed to Zarkashī. After 578 (1182/3) according to Ibn Abī Zar', *Rawḍ al-qirṭās*, ed. C. J. Tornberg in *Annales regum Mauritaniae* (Uppsala, 1843-46), I, p. ١٣٥. On the chronology of Ibn Rushd's life at this period see S. Munk, *Mélanges de philosophie juive et arabe* (Paris, 1859), pp. 422-24; E. Renan, *Averroès*, pp. 18-19; L. Gauthier, *Ibn Rochd*, pp. 8-9. But the subject needs working out afresh on the basis of all the surviving evidence.

[3] See E. I. J. Rosenthal, *Averroës' Commentary on Plato's Republic* (Cambridge, 1956), Introduction, pp. 10-11. The place of publication of the two commentaries and our three treatises is not recorded. In 574 (1178/9) a portion of the *De substantia orbis* was completed in Marrākush: *Aristotelis opera omnia . . . Averrois Cordubensis . . . Commentaria* (Venice, 1560), V, p. 327.

[4] p. 28.

large section of the public.[1] There is more evidence from this period,[2] but it would be wearisome to go further. It is sufficient to note that *Faṣl al-maqāl* is itself the best evidence of the prevailing unpopularity of philosophy, for though it is outwardly confident and even aggressive, it is essentially a work of defence such as would not have been thought necessary in the days of the older philosophers.

It is a reasonable guess that it was the writing and publication of the Aristotelian commentaries themselves which in the 70's aroused the usual murmurs against this pagan science, useless speculation and source of corruption to honest Muslims. To these complaints Ibn Rushd could not avoid giving a direct answer. And he was exceptionally well qualified to do so, by reason of his mastery of both law and philosophy, his probable position as a *qāḍī* at the time, and the patronage of the prince.

The main conclusions of the last two sections, then, may be summed up as follows. In *Faṣl al-maqāl*, Ibn Rushd was primarily giving a legal retort to a condemnation of philosophy that had been spelled out by Ghazālī and was now being pressed in the West by Ash'arite schoolmen. The reading public to whom the work is addressed may be presumed to have consisted largely of Andalusians educated in the Malikite legal tradition. Thus, while the work displays direct antagonism to Ash'arite theology, its attitude to this public is one of persuasion, using legal arguments about philosophy and parallels between philosophy and jurisprudence.

The attitude of Ibn Rushd towards the Almohad religious movement would be better known to us if his commentary on Ibn Tūmart's Creed, *'Aqīdat at-tawḥīd*, had survived.[3] We can certainly assume that he was hostile to the Ash'arite elements in Ibn Tūmart's theology, but it seems unlikely that he would be able to attack the ideas of the Mahdī directly, even though the present prince, Abū Ya'qūb, was privately no longer a strict follower of those ideas. In the *Commentary on Plato's Republic* the ruling monarch is referred to as a philosopher king[4] and praised as the patron of the writer;[5] this is only natural and seems quite

[1] Ibn Abī Uṣaybi'a, *'Uyūn al-anbā'*, II, p. 69 (life of Abū Bakr Ibn Zuhr) and 76-77 (life of Ibn Rushd); Ibn al-Abbār, *Takmila*, p. 270; Anṣārī, fragment of Life of Ibn Rushd in E. Renan, *Averroès*, pp. 437-47; Dhahabī, Life of Abū Yūsuf in E. Renan, *Averroès*, pp. 460-62; Marrākushī, *Mu'jib*, pp. 223-25.

[2] E.g. Ibn Abī Uṣaybi'a, *'Uyūn al-anbā'*, II, pp. 69-70 (life of Abū Bakr Ibn Zuhr); Ibn Ṭufayl, *Ḥayy Ibn Yaqẓān*, pp. ١٥٠-٥١; Maqqarī, *Nafḥ aṭ-ṭīb* (Cairo, 1949), I, pp. 205-6.

[3] This commentary is listed in Escurial, MS. 879 in Casiri's catalogue, fol. 82: in E. Renan, *Averroès*, p. 464. See I. Goldziher, Introduction to *Ibn Toumert*, pp. 79-82.

[4] II, iii, 1-2 and xvii, 3.

[5] III, xxi, 1.

unforced. Mention is made, however, of the ruler's lack of influence over the beliefs of the public,[1] which are said to be dominated by "the sophists", i.e. the theologians.[2] There is a favourable reference to the dynasty at the end of *Faṣl*, if I have rightly interpreted the phrase *hādh al-amr al-ghālib*;[3] and *Faṣl* is in line with royal views both in its defence of philosophy and in its attitude to popular religious education. This is not to say that *Faṣl* was written at the royal command. Ibn Rushd states explicitly that it was only written in reaction to the publicity that the issue had received, and that otherwise he would have been most reluctant to discuss such questions outside scientific circles.[4] This is sufficient proof that the treatise was written on his own initiative.

A somewhat similar relation prevailed between Ibn Rushd and Ibn Ṭufayl. Ibn Rushd was not a disciple of Ibn Ṭufayl, and nowhere refers to his philosophic ideas.[5] But on the questions of *Faṣl*, Ibn Ṭufayl's *Ḥayy Ibn Yaqẓān* (published a few years before or after *Faṣl*) presents the same views though in a less developed form. Doubtless these questions were discussed between the two philosophers in the presence of the prince.

THE PROBLEM OF THE BOOK

The contents of *Faṣl al-maqāl* have been much discussed over the last fifty years, in the course of a distinguished debate among scholars—Asín and Gauthier, Horten, Alonso, Allard and others.[6] The debate has for the most part been concerned with Ibn Rushd's attitude to Islam, a broad question which requires for its answer a consideration of far more than the present treatise. To review the previous literature, or to offer an opinion on the general question, would call for a discussion disproportionate to this introduction. The following sections will be confined to an account of *Faṣl*, with

[1] II, xvii, 3.
[2] II, iv, 5.
[3] p. 26, line 10. See note 196 to the translation.
[4] 18. 16-18.
[5] On the relation of the two as philosophers see L. Gauthier, Introduction to *Hayy ben Yaqdhân, roman philosophique d'Ibn Thofaïl*, 2nd ed. (Beirut, 1936), pp. 121-28.
[6] The most important contributions, in chronological order: M. Asín Palacios, "El averroismo teologico de Santo Tomás de Aquino", in *Homenaje á D. Francisco Codera* (Saragossa, 1904), pp. 271-331; L. Gauthier, *La théorie d'Ibn Rochd (Averroès) sur les rapports de la religion et de la philosophie* (Paris, 1909); M. Horten, *Texte zu dem Streite zwischen Glauben und Wissen im Islam* (Bonn, 1913), and the review of it by A. Bonucci in *Rivista degli Studi Orientali*, **1** (1916), pp. 508-15; L. Gauthier, "Scolastique musulmane et scolastique chrétienne", *Revue d'Histoire de la Philosophie*, **2** (1928), pp. 221-53, 333-65; L. Gauthier, *Ibn Rochd (Averroès): Traité décisif*, 2nd ed. (Algiers, 1942), pp. ix-xxii; M. Alonso, *Teología de Averroes* (Madrid-Granada, 1947), pp. 99-118; L. Gauthier, *Ibn Rochd (Averroès)* (Paris, 1948), ch. 2; M. Allard, "Le rationalisme d'Averroès d'après une étude sur la création", *Bulletin d'Études Orientales*, **14** (1952-54), pp. 7-59.

a view to bringing out its main features and answering some questions that naturally arise about it.[1] In the process I shall resume many points that have now been established, and make such additions and modifications as have occurred to me in the course of study.

We should start by noticing carefully what the work is about, in order to avoid some misconceptions that can easily arise. Ibn Rushd, in his usual manner, states the purpose of the treatise at the very beginning: it is "to examine, from the standpoint of the study of the Law (*an-naẓar ash-sharʿī*), whether the study of philosophy (*an-naẓar fil-falsafa*) and logic is allowed by the Law (*ash-sharʿ*), or prohibited, or commanded—either by way of recommendation or as obligatory" (p. 1). Thus the question is formulated as one of Islamic law: in which of the legal categories must philosophic activity be placed? The answer which follows in the rest of the book is derived from the two scriptural sources of law, the *Qur'ān* and the Traditions, and the two further accepted principles, consensus (*ijmāʿ*) and reasoning (*qiyās*). Thus the whole treatise must be classed as legal in the Islamic sense; or it may equally be said, in modern terms, that it deals with a moral question. The subject whose status is in question is philosophy, but the treatise itself is not a philosophical work; it is a legal treatise *about* philosophy. And Ibn Rushd writes it in his capacity as a legal theorist and practising judge, though the fact that he is also a practising philosopher makes a great difference to his conclusions, as will be shown.

We may next examine the two terms that enter into this legal relation. The final judicial arbiter is said to be the *sharʿ*. I have translated this term as "Scripture" whenever it refers primarily to a text, an object of study, and as "Law" when it refers rather to a source of commands and prohibitions to man. In the Arabic word both concepts are bound together: *sharʿ* is Lawgiving Scripture or Scriptural Law. The Scripture referred to is primarily the *Qur'ān* and secondarily the Traditions; the ultimate Lawgiver is God, through the mouth and deeds of His Prophet Muḥammad (who is also referred to as "the lawgiver", *ash-shāriʿ*).[2] But the Prophet is dead, and Scripture does not speak or judge; there is thus inevitably a continuing human element in legal decision—collective, through the doctrine of *ijmāʿ*, and personal, in so far as the judge has a residue of discretion to interpret Scripture. Nevertheless, though Ibn Rushd later in the book defends the philosopher's analogous right to use such limited discretion in his own

[1] I have inserted detailed summaries in the translation.

[2] *Faṣl* 22, following a practice of Fārābī and Ibn Sīnā. See n. 171 to the translation.

field, he does not question the truth and authority of Scripture nor the framework of Islamic legal theory within which all judgements are to be given. We should therefore accept the fact that he starts from the Law, and view the work primarily from its own standpoint.

The other term is the object to be judged, the study of philosophy (*an-naẓar fil-falsafa*). This is an activity, not a set of books or a particular philosophic system. The question is not about the works of Aristotle but about the occupation of contemporary philosophers, such as the author and his colleagues in Andalus. *Naẓar* means theoretical, scientific study (Greek *theōria*): it is misleading to translate it as "speculation", with its modern connotations of uncertain methods and conclusions. *Falsafa* is shortly to be defined by Ibn Rushd, in the first pages of his answer, so I shall leave the consideration of its meaning to the next section.

The General Solution

Ibn Rushd's answer to his problem falls naturally into three main parts, which I have designated as chapters. In Chapter 1 (pp. 1-7) he gives an initial answer, without yet facing the major difficulties. This answer is deduced from Scripture by a regular juristic argument.

Many passages of the *Qur'ān* bid man to observe and reflect on the natural universe, in order to recognize the manifestations of God's power in it. Thus "the Law has rendered obligatory the study of beings by the intellect, and reflection on them" (p. 2). This step provides the necessary textual basis of the argument. It is a fact that the *Qur'ān* is full of exhortations to observation and reflection on the power of God in the world, though it is not clear how Ibn Rushd has inferred obligation rather than recommendation from the passages quoted.

The next step is to show that this observation and reflection on the universe at its best (as it obviously should be) involves a study of philosophy, for the systematic application of demonstrative reasoning to the world is philosophy.

Two points here call for explanation and criticism. (1) Philosophy is conceived as a demonstrative science. *Falsafa* is the Greek *philosophia*, philosophy in the Greek tradition. It is thought of by Ibn Rushd and his Arabic predecessors not as speculative in the modern sense, but as yielding a knowledge of reality which is demonstrative according to the Aristotelian conditions: conclusions drawn by flawless logic from indubitable premisses. Philosophy is thus thought of as a kind of science, giving certain truth to the qualified philosopher who reasons with sufficient care.

It shares with the other sciences the authoritative name of *ḥikma* (wisdom, Greek *sophia*), and this name is more often used than *falsafa* in *Faṣl*.[1]

It is this characterization of philosophy as demonstrative science which provides the key to Ibn Rushd's whole position in *Faṣl*. Accordingly we must ask what truth there is in it. It might be objected that philosophy in its proper sense, as we understand it today, is not a science at all because it is carefully separated both from mathematics and from the empirical sciences. However that may be—and the proper definition of philosophy is still in dispute—it would provide merely a verbal criticism of Ibn Rushd; for he is talking of *falsafa*, and this does contain elements of "natural philosophy" which we now classify as empirical science. And science is at any rate a rational, organized study of the universe.

But just when science is empirical, it cannot be demonstrative. We can never have indubitable premisses about any part of the empirical world, let alone the cosmos as a whole. This dilemma—either demonstrative or empirical, but not both—has become clear to most thinkers in modern times, but it was not so to a mediaeval Aristotelian: for him all sciences, including philosophy, started from indubitable first principles.

(2) Ibn Rushd, in his opening statement, sets out to prove that philosophy[2] is *nothing more* than teleological study of the world. But philosophy in mediaeval Islam went considerably beyond such a study. Leaving out logic, which was considered as an instrument of philosophy rather than part of it, we still have the greater portions of physical philosophy and psychology, ethics, political philosophy and metaphysics—those portions which were not simply intended to prove God's power but were studied for their own interest or with a view to man's happiness. And in his main conclusion (pp. 4-5) what Ibn Rushd establishes is only that the *Qur'ān* encourages a scientific, teleological study of the world, which is a part of philosophy.

But, in fact, there is nothing in the Book which forbids other kinds of study, such as the remainder of philosophy. Ibn Rushd should have proved by the negative way the *permissibility* of *all* philosophy, which was after all the practical goal that had to be assured in his environment. He has neglected this task, and pushed ahead to claim an *obligation* to study a *part* of philosophy. His procedure is one example of a certain aggressiveness which characterizes the treatise.

From the general position he has reached, Ibn Rushd proceeds to make further inferences: that logic is necessary as a tool, that

[1] See L. Gauthier, *La théorie*, p. 46.

[2] "Philosophy" will normally mean *falsafa* or *ḥikma* unless I indicate otherwise.

this tool can be efficiently acquired only from the ancient Greeks, and that philosophy proper can be efficiently practised only after learning ancient Greek philosophy. These conclusions follow very easily. He merely has to parry conservative objections to these studies as being a heretical innovation (*bid'a*), pagan in origin, and harmful to some people. In answering these objections he uses analogical arguments, comparing logic and philosophy with other lawful practices (use of non-Muslim instruments, pp. 3-4), and with the science of Islamic jurisprudence itself. From the frequency of the legal analogies in this part (five in pp. 2-7), it is plain that the author is addressing himself to an audience of lawyers, or at least to persons interested in the law.

In the course of showing that the harm that philosophy sometimes causes is accidental, he brings in a new point: that philosophy should only be studied by people who are qualified to use demonstrative arguments. This point is developed a little where he speaks of three methods of acquiring religious knowledge, suitable for three classes of minds. The scheme becomes important in the later parts of the book.

The structure of Chapter 1 is clear. In a few pages Ibn Rushd has arrived swiftly and boldly at his main conclusion: that philosophy, including study of Greek philosophy, is sanctioned by the *Qur'ān*. Not a very welcome conclusion to the '*ulamā*' of Andalus! But the real difficulties have still to appear.

ALLEGORICAL INTERPRETATION OF SCRIPTURE

Chapter 2 (pp. 7-18) contains answers to major objections to Ibn Rushd's thesis. These objections form a logical series, each one arising out of the answer to the one before.

The *prima facie* objection is that philosophy taught doctrines about God and the world which were at variance with the teachings of Scripture: it could not then be a study that Scripture commanded, or even permitted. This is the familiar accusation of the Muslim theologians against philosophy in the pagan Greek tradition. It is not explicitly stated here by Ibn Rushd, but it is clearly implied in his general answer, which is given in the first sentence of Chapter 2. "Now since this religion is true and summons to the study which leads to knowledge of the Truth, we the Muslim community know definitely that demonstrative study does not lead to [conclusions] conflicting with what Scripture has given us; for truth does not oppose truth but accords with it and bears witness to it" (p. 7).

It must be noted that there would have been no problem if Ibn Rushd had held such a theory of "double truth" as was imputed to him in Latin circles in the thirteenth century. Revealed truths would have been true "in the religious realm" and those of the world "in the philosophic realm", and no contradiction could have arisen between them. It is just because he held a unitary view of truth that a problem arises. Scripture makes assertions about the same world of fact as that of philosophy; therefore a conflict between them is conceivable, if either of them has made false assertions.

His bold *a priori* answer quoted above is inevitable when once it is granted that Scripture and philosophy are both reliable sources of the same kind of truth: factual, descriptive truth about an objective world. Ibn Rushd here raises no question about the truthfulness of either source; for in *Faṣl* he has taken Scripture as his starting-point, and he has not chosen to defend the truths of philosophy philosophically, but deferred that task to *Tahāfut at-tahāfut* which he wrote a few years later. Assuming, then, that the statements of both sources are really true, no real contradiction can arise, and Ibn Rushd can make this assertion in the above sweeping sentence, which is in a sense the central statement of the treatise.

The real concern of *Faṣl*, then, is something else: it is to show that *apparent* contradictions between Scripture and philosophy can be reconciled, i.e. explained away by a method that is legitimate according to the Law. To this task Ibn Rushd proceeds straightway.

After isolating what he takes to be the real problem, apparent conflicts between some statements of Scripture and philosophy, he describes the method of reconciliation: allegorical interpretation (*ta'wīl*) of the apparent meaning (*ẓāhir*) of Scripture, in such a fashion that the inner meaning of Scripture is seen to agree with demonstrative truth. The nature of the method of *ta'wīl* as conceived by Ibn Rushd is of such crucial importance for his position that it deserves further examination. I shall draw upon statements and implications from various parts of *Faṣl* and *Manāhij* in order to arrive at a clear view of his theory.

Ibn Rushd defines *ta'wīl* as "extension of the significance of an expression from real to metaphorical significance, without forsaking therein the standard metaphorical practices of Arabic, such as calling a thing by the name of something resembling it or a cause or consequence or accompaniment of it, or other things such as are enumerated in accounts of the kinds of metaphorical speech" (p. 7). But this definition does not carry us far towards answering the most important questions. Linguistic rules can only set limits, within which several alternative interpretations of a sentence or passage may be possible. How do we determine whether to interpret allegorically at all, and if so what precise interpretation to adopt? To judge the right level of interpretation, Ibn Rushd accepts an elaborate system of rules expounded by Ghazālī: according to it there are five possible levels of meaning, and *ta'wīl* of a passage or sentence of Scripture to a deeper meaning is only permitted if a more literal meaning is proved to be impossible.[1] Impossibility is indicated if the passage is in apparent contradiction with another more authoritative passage of the *Qur'ān*; since the *Qur'ān* does not contradict itself, the former passage must be interpreted allegorically, at the first level that reconciles it with the latter.

These rules provide some check upon rash and arbitrary interpretation. But still something further is needed: a criterion to decide what is the precise allegorical interpretation to be selected, when several are possible at the same level. How do we know what makes the best sense of a passage? Only by a science which gives true information about the world: namely philosophy! This conclusion is not stated, but it is implied by Ibn Rushd's assertions that the people who have the right to interpret Scripture allegorically are the demonstrative scholars, i.e. the philosophers (pp. 7, 10). For why are they alone qualified? The answer must be that in their knowledge of nature they have a principle for selection of the true inner meaning of Scripture: it is that which corresponds with the reality known by philosophy.[2]

Thus philosophers are set up as judges of the meaning of Scripture. Theologians (the *mutakallimūn*—Mu'tazilites and Ash'arites) are incompetent because they can only attain dialectical reasoning which starts from popularly accepted premisses. They are incapable of sound *ta'wīl* because they do not possess the qualifications of demonstrative science. Such ideas were dangerous to their author in the environment of western Islam; but they are inevitable *when once philosophy is admitted as demonstrative science*, giving knowledge of reality. This is a key idea which explains most of what Ibn Rushd has to say on the relations of philosophy with Scripture. (A striking illustration of its importance is furnished by his attempt to give Scriptural authority to this concept of philosophy. He invokes for this purpose the verse of the *Qur'ān* (iii, 5) which speaks of *ar-rāsikhūn fil-'ilm*, "those who are well grounded in learning", and argues that what distinguishes them must be their demonstrative knowledge (p. 10). But there is no proof given that this is the kind of knowledge referred to by the *Qur'ān*, and if it is, there is again no proof that philosophy fulfils the requirements of demonstrative knowledge. Thus the interpretation of the passage is itself determined by the philosopher's assumptions that demonstrative knowledge is the highest kind and that philosophy is demonstrative.)

[1] *Faṣl*, 15; *Manāhij*, 125. Ghazālī, *Fayṣal*, in *Jawāhir*, pp. 80-82.

[2] I do not find this answer explicitly stated; but, as I have said, it is the only possible explanation of why the philosophers are uniquely qualified for *ta'wīl*. See below, p. 27, for a criticism of this part of Ibn Rushd's theory.

As a check on the other procedures, Ibn Rushd suggests a further criterion of whether an allegorical interpretation is correct: that if it is it will always be confirmed by the apparent meaning of another passage, i.e. by a direct statement elsewhere in Scripture (p. 8). But this procedure is only mentioned once, with the air of an afterthought; and it is doubtful whether Ibn Rushd could have applied it convincingly to a large proportion of cases.

A number of critical questions will readily occur to modern readers about Ibn Rushd's theory of allegorical interpretation. In answering these I hope to provide a better understanding of his position.

(1) Does he set up Aristotle as another Scripture, and thus merely substitute one authority for another? The answer to this is No, for two reasons. In the first place there is no question of substitution: philosophy is only one of the two main bases of interpretation, as has been shown, and I see no reason to doubt Ibn Rushd's sincerity with regard to the other, linguistic usage. Secondly, although his veneration for Aristotle is very great (as may be seen both in his commentaries and in his *Tahāfut*), it is not a veneration for authority as such, but only a respect for the Sage as a medium of truth about the world. From his own scientific observations Ibn Rushd occasionally goes beyond or criticizes statements of Aristotle.[1]

His general attitude to him is well defined in Chapter 1 of *Faṣl*: if we have predecessors who have made great progress in knowledge of reality, we should be foolish to ignore what they have given us, though we may add a little in each succeeding generation. Here again we see his conception of philosophy as a science resting on sure foundations, not as speculation which may be overthrown entirely by new thoughts. Scripture must agree with philosophy only in so far as the latter gives true knowledge of reality.

(2) Ibn Rushd starts out ostensibly from the *shar*ʿ but then he sets up the philosophers as judges of the meaning of the *shar*ʿ. Is this procedure impious in relation to Islam: disrespectful of Scripture or of duly constituted religious authorities? No, it is not; for someone must interpret the *shar*ʿ, and, within the limits imposed by *ijmā*ʿ (to be explained in the following section), authority to interpret is the privilege of the most competent. In practical matters the authority of the *fuqahā*' was never questioned. But in matters of doctrine there were no finally recognized authorities, at least in twelfth-century Andalus. The criteria of competence themselves depended on the criteria for correct interpretation. To a philosopher like Ibn Rushd, agreement with philosophic truth was a

[1] See Alonso, pp. 25-41; M. Allard, "Le rationalisme d'Averroès".

necessary criterion: from this it followed inevitably that only people with philosophic knowledge were competent to interpret. And this view was as permissible as any other.

(3) When there is a contradiction between the apparent meanings of a true Scripture and a true philosophy, why is it always Scripture which has to yield and be interpreted allegorically? Is it because Ibn Rushd has more confidence in the accuracy of philosophy? No, it is because of a difference in the manner in which the two sources express truth. Philosophy in the Aristotelian tradition is prosaic and direct, being a kind of science. There is thus absolutely no room for finding in it hidden, allegorical meanings. The *Qur'ān* on the other hand is imaginative and may be made to yield hidden treasures; and this is not a fault in Ibn Rushd's eyes, it is a quality in which "the precious Book" excels every other (p. 25). (In Western terms we should say that the *Qur'ān* is poetic, with all the advantages of poetry implied, but Ibn Rushd could not say this on account of the *Qur'ān*'s own rejection of that attribute.)

(4) If philosophers can arrive at the truth directly, is Scripture unnecessary to them? Yes, at the highest level. This is a matter on which the Islamic philosophers were necessarily discreet. But Ibn Rushd's general position implies that he would assent, at least in part, to one of the conclusions of Ibn Ṭufayl's fable: " . . . Asāl did not doubt that all the things that had been revealed in his Scripture concerning God, Great and Glorious, His angels, His books, His prophets, the last day, His paradise and His hell-fire, were images (*amthila*) of these things which Ḥayy Ibn Yaqẓān had seen (*shāhadahā*)", by his unaided intellect.[1] But the ordinary philosopher, unlike Ḥayy, grows up amid the distractions and temptations of society, and before he attains the goals of philosophy he needs Scripture to help him on his way. In his youth he needs the moral education which is the indispensable basis for philosophy. This is best provided by Scripture,[2] which works on the adolescent imagination and builds up sound habits as prescribed in the pedagogical theories of Plato and Aristotle. At a more advanced stage of education, philosophic minds are stimulated by the apparent contradictions and obscurities in the *Qur'ān*, and thus led on to the inner meanings which contain the truth (pp. 8, 25).

Moreover, a single passage of *Tahāfut at-tahāfut*[3] suggests that revelation provides certain truths beyond the range of any intellect to know; but the passage is somewhat ambiguous and I believe

[1] *Ḥayy Ibn Yaqẓān*, p. ١٤٤. See also below, pp. 33-34, for Ibn Rushd's view of Scripture as partially fable.

[2] *Tahāfut at-tahāfut*, ed. M. Bouyges, in *Bibliotheca Arabica Scholasticorum*, III (Beirut, 1930), pp. 527, 582-84.

[3] pp. 255-56.

Ibn Rushd is not being altogether frank in his statement on this point.[1]

(5) It may be suggested that if agreement with philosophy is made one of the criteria for the correct interpretation of Scripture, the meaning of Scripture is prejudged. Does the *Qur'ān* really say the same things as Greek philosophy, or has Ibn Rushd arbitrarily "cooked" his results, predetermining the *Qur'ān*'s meaning by a requirement that is extrinsic to it? These questions cannot easily be answered without a special study of his particular interpretations, though it can hardly be denied that some of them are forced—e.g. on the resurrection.[2] It is easy for us to see the weaknesses, because we are detached and do not regard Aristotelian science as the last word on reality. We can see real gaps between Greek philosophy and the *Qur'ān*. But Ibn Rushd was facing the dilemma of all religious modernists, who accept as true both a Scripture and the science of their day. In this situation the best he could do was to face the problem, and find interpretations of his Scripture which satisfied the requirements of harmony with philosophy without doing too much violence to the linguistic properties of the text. In this he has probably done as well as could be expected.

To conclude this section I shall contrast Ibn Rushd's method of interpretation with that of two other groups in mediaeval Islam, the mystics and the Ash'arites.

Ghazālī in writing of *ta'wīl* says that the extent to which it should be practised is obscure and hard to determine, except for "those who grasp things by a divine Light not by hearsay. Then when the mysteries of things are revealed to them as they really are, they inquire into Tradition and the revealed words: and whatever agrees with what they have witnessed by the light of certainty, they accept, and whatever disagrees they interpret allegorically".[3] Like Ibn Rushd, Ghazālī sets up an extrinsic standard of interpretation; but in place of an objective, demonstrative science he puts personal mystical experience. The dangers of arbitrary manipulation of the sacred text would seem even greater in such a system. Yet, according to H. Corbin's account,[4] mystical *ta'wīl* has another characteristic which makes it less arbitrary or not so at all: this is that in it the symbol is the only possible expression of the symbolized, which is a personal experience existing on another level than rational truth. It is clear that Ibn Rushd's conception has nothing to do with this

[1] M. Asín Palacios, in *Homenaje*, p. 281, accepts the statement at its face value. L. Gauthier would certainly not have done so, but I have not encountered an explanation of this passage by him.

[2] *Manāhij*, 122-23.

[3] *Iḥyā' 'ulūm ad-dīn*, 'Irāqī ed. (Cairo, 1938-39), I, p. 180.

[4] *Avicenne et le récit visionnaire* (Teheran, 1954), II, pp. 32 ff.; and more briefly in his introduction to Nāṣir-e Khosraw, p. 66.

one. It is rational through and through, and the *bāṭin* is a fact capable of description in the same sense as the *ẓāhir*. Thus no doubt his *ẓāhir* is properly described as allegory, following Corbin's definition of allegory as artificial figuration of abstract generalizations, which could equally well be represented otherwise.[1] He even denies that the Ṣūfīs attain a genuine union with the divine (the basis of experience required for mystical interpretation), since knowledge of the theoretical sciences is the only road to union, and they do not possess such knowledge.[2]

Between Ibn Rushd and the Ash'arites there is not such an absolute difference about the method of interpretation. Both admit some allegory in Scripture, and both go beyond linguistic rules in determining when and how Scripture should be interpreted allegorically: the Ash'arites on the basis of certain theological principles, Ibn Rushd on the basis of the system of Greco-Arabic philosophy. Where they differ is in the value they attach to scientific and philosophical knowledge. To the Ash'arites, the consistency of Scripture with modern scientific truth was a secondary requirement, compared with the correct understanding of Scripture in its Arabic context and in the light of their own system of theology. This attitude led to their atomic theory of time and matter and their denial of natural causality, positions which were castigated as absurd by Ben Maymōn and Ibn Rushd. Ben Maymōn wrote that "the earlier theologians, both of the Greek Christians and of the Mohammedans, when they laid down their propositions, did not investigate the real properties of things; first of all they considered what must be the properties of the things which should yield proof for or against a certain creed; and when this was found they asserted that the thing must be endowed with those properties".[3] With Ibn Rushd it was otherwise: he had to accommodate the meaning of Scripture to the scientific truth about the world. He takes far more seriously than the Ash'arites the fact that we have direct, objective knowledge of the world, not gained through Scripture but through science in the broad sense (*ḥikma*), including philosophy.

IJMĀ' AND THE FREEDOM OF PHILOSOPHY

In the last section some objections were considered that occur readily to modern minds. But these objections are not those which Ibn Rushd is directly concerned to answer. He is concerned pri-

[1] *Ibid.*, pp. 34 and 66 respectively.

[2] *Talkhīs kitāb an-nafs* (= *Summary of De Animā*), ed. A. F. Ahwānī (Cairo, 1950), p. 95; *Manāhij*, 41-42.

[3] *Guide*, Part 1, ch. 71: Eng. tr. M. Friedländer, 2nd ed., p. 109; cf. Fārābī, *Iḥṣā' al-'ulūm*, 2nd ed. U. M. Amīn (Cairo, 1948), pp. 110-13; L. Gauthier, "Scolastique musulmane et scolastique chrétienne", pp. 349-50.

marily with one which has a mediaeval ring and is remote from our thoughts today. This is that some of the interpretations of Scripture given by the philosophers are unorthodox and must be condemned as unbelief (*kufr*). Such a condemnation would carry very serious penalities for philosophers: not merely destruction of their books and a ban on their teaching, but exclusion from the Muslim community and loss of legal protection of person and property. It is likely that a legal condemnation of this sort was being talked about, and Ibn Rushd sets out to forestall it in legal terms (pp. 8-17).

Orthodoxy in Islam has never been defined by ecclesiastical councils, as in Christianity.[1] No such councils have ever been held, owing to the absence of an ordained priesthood in Islam. But orthodoxy has been defined in terms of acceptance by the Islamic community, whose consensus (*ijmāʿ*) cannot be erroneous; conversely, unorthodox practice or doctrine is that which is contrary to *ijmāʿ*. Even the genuineness and truth of the existing text of the *Qur'ān* were only confirmed, in the last analysis, by *ijmāʿ*: hence it provides the ultimate authority for the entire system of Islamic law, as has often been pointed out.

But the simple conception of *ijmāʿ* was vague and required further precision. It was impossible to consider the opinions of every Muslim; in practice, therefore, *ijmāʿ* meant the consensus of the learned (the *ʿulamā'*). These were more particularly the most venerated scholars of Islamic law and theology of the first two centuries. On matters of conduct, *ijmāʿ* had determined a large part of Islamic law by the death of the fourth great *imām* of the law schools, Aḥmad Ibn Ḥanbal (d. 855). On matters of doctrine, however, there was too much variety among the learned to allow *ijmāʿ* to proceed very far, and the situation remained somewhat fluid for several centuries more, until the Ashʿarites, the Shiʿite theologians or others were able to establish a practical conformity in the several countries where they prevailed. Ibn Rushd in *Faṣl* is fighting against the imposition of such a conformity in doctrine by the Ashʿarites of his time and place, and defending the freedom of the small minority of the philosophers.

The crucial issue is rapidly narrowed down (p. 8). The question concerns the right of qualified philosophers to interpret Scripture according to their personal judgement. There is already *ijmāʿ* on two classes of texts in Scripture: those which all agree must be taken in their literal meaning, and those which all agree must be interpreted allegorically. But there is a third class of texts about which there has not been any *ijmāʿ*. It is admitted by all scholars

[1] See L. Gauthier, "Scolastique musulmane et scolastique chrétienne", pp. 340ff.

that such a third class exists, but its extent is a matter of dispute. Thus philosophers are accused of understanding allegorically certain texts, which their opponents consider to belong to the first class. If this accusation is correct they will be guilty of violating *ijmā'*, and hence of unbelief.

Ibn Rushd accepts the general authority of *ijmā'*, and the legal consequence that disregarding it is *kufr*, with one qualification: the *ijmā'* must be historically established with certainty. But if *ijmā'* is only presumed and probable, then it is not right to give a decision of *kufr* against one who disregards it. For this position he cites the opinion of the leading Ash'arite theorists themselves, Abul-Ma'ālī al-Juwaynī and Ghazālī (p. 8)[1].

The qualification mentioned above provides the basis of his argument on behalf of the philosophers. He first gives a general answer: that historical certainty about *ijmā'* is never attained in relation to matters of doctrine. After listing the conditions that must be satisfied to establish such certainty, he argues that one of them has not been fulfilled at any period in the past. This is the condition that the true opinion of all the scholars must be known; and it has never been satisfied because there have always been Muslim scholars who have, on principle, concealed their true opinion on matters of doctrine except to an inner circle of disciples and associates (pp. 9-10).

Yet Ghazālī in his *Tahāfut al-falāsifa* had condemned Fārābī and Ibn Sīnā as *kāfirs* on account of three of their opinions (see below). Ibn Rushd thinks that, in view of Ghazālī's legal position in his *Fayṣal at-tafriqa*, he could not have meant his condemnation as a definite legal verdict (*bil-qaṭ'*), but must have meant it in a more tentative sense (pp. 9-10).

After the general answer to the charge of *kufr*, Ibn Rushd goes on to defend the philosophers on the particular counts on which they were accused. If the general answer is correct, the particular answers should be unnecessary; but Ibn Rushd gives them anyway, presumably as a second line of defence. On each of the three questions he gives a brief argument, not going into the philosophical issues more deeply than is needed to make the legal defence. And each argument is of a different kind.

In answer to the accusation that the philosophers say that God does not know particulars, Ibn Rushd denies the fact. What they really say is that He does not know particulars in the same way as men do (pp. 10-11).[2] It should be noted that he refers to the

[1] Yet in *Manāhij*, 72, he criticizes Ghazālī for permitting defiance of *ijmā'*, without mentioning Ghazālī's acceptance of *ijmā'* in principle. Ghazālī, *Fayṣal*, pp. 87-89.

[2] See *Ḍamīma* for a fuller discussion of the philosophical problem.

Peripatetics—Aristotle and his Greek followers; as in *Tahāfut at-tahāfut*, Ibn Rushd does not mind what is said about his Arabic predecessors so long as the pure Aristotelian doctrine is cleared.

Concerning the philosophers' assertion that the world is eternal, he argues that (even if accusations of *kufr* in these matters are possible) the difference between the philosophic and Ash'arite positions is in reality too slight to warrant such accusations (pp. 11-13). He analyses the positions of the two parties, using an "ordinary language" method, of the type brought into prominence in our day by Wittgenstein, Ryle and their contemporaries in England. Thus Ibn Rushd explains that the origin of the world has certain characteristics which belong to what we normally call "pre-eternal", and others which belong to what we normally call "created". Therefore "the disagreement between the Ash'arite theologians and the ancient philosophers is in my view almost resolvable into a disagreement about naming" (p. 11).

There is also a supplementary argument, to the effect that the apparent meaning of the *Qur'ān* in its statements on the origin of the world coincides with the doctrine of the philosophers: it apparently affirms a creation of the world, but not *ex nihilo*: so it is the Ash'arites who interpret the *Qur'ān* allegorically! And it is impossible for them to claim that this interpretation is backed by *ijmā'*, since one group of Muslim scholars, the philosophers, do not accept it (p. 13). (A significant claim is made here in passing: that the Arabic philosophers are a group of Muslim *'ulamā'* whose agreement is necessary to establish *ijmā'*.)

With regard to the third position of the philosophers, the denial of bodily resurrection, Ibn Rushd's defence is notably more cautious. He starts by providing a new basis of defence (pp. 13-16). Instead of asking, What beliefs has the Muslim community agreed to outlaw?, he sets up a more absolute criterion for deciding what is unbelief: the question now is, What kinds of error in belief will not be excused by God? Ibn Rushd expounds his answer rather elaborately, but its central principle is simple: God will not excuse errors in interpretation where He has made Scripture perfectly intelligible to people, according to their intellectual levels. (Here he brings in the theory of intellectual classes, but I shall postpone consideration of it to the next section.) But where there is reasonable cause for doubt about the meaning of a text, and where a man is qualified to exercise his judgement about it, he will be excused if his considered judgement is in error.

This conclusion is supported in two ways, Scriptural and Aristotelian. Ibn Rushd quotes the familiar Tradition, "If the judge after exerting his mind (*ijtahada*) makes a right decision, he will have a double reward; and if he makes a wrong decision he will [still] have a single reward", and he extends its application from decisions in law to decisions in science. The philosophic justification for the view lies in an inference from Aristotle's theory of the relations of the will and the intellect: that when once we have arrived at a conclusion after an exhaustive intellectual inquiry, we have no choice but to accept the conclusion. And having no choice we are not blameable if we make a mistake.[1]

The new criterion is now applied to the philosophers' interpretations of the Scriptural texts about the next life (pp. 16-17). Ibn Rushd admits that it is unbelief to deny the broad dogma that there is some kind of future life, because Scripture makes it clear to all classes of men. (The philosophic arguments for a future life are not called for in *Faṣl.*) But various views can reasonably be held about the nature of the next life: that we are resurrected with some kind of bodies or in our souls alone.[2] Error on this matter by qualified scholars is therefore excusable. (Moreover, since various views actually *are* held, there is no *ijmāʿ* on it: "there is disagreement"—p. 16.)

The upshot of these last pages (pp. 10-17) is that Muslim philosophers are free to believe that God knows particulars only in a special sense, that the world is eternal, and that resurrection is of the soul alone. All these doctrines were an essential part of Islamic Aristotelianism.

Before leaving the whole subject, however, Ibn Rushd states emphatically that such doctrines and the corresponding interpretations of Scripture ought to be confined strictly, on pain of *takfīr*, to learned circles and not revealed to the public (pp. 17-18). He blames Ghazālī for publishing such matters in popular works; he excuses himself for referring to these matters in *Faṣl*, on the ground that they had already received publicity. These two pages form a transition to the next chapter, where the question of publicity for philosophy becomes the primary subject.

Restrictions on Explaining Allegories

In Chapter 2 Ibn Rushd has upheld the philosophers' right to interpret Scripture allegorically, but made it conditional upon their competence in demonstrative reasoning, which is essential to understanding the inner meaning of Scripture. In Chapter 3 (pp. 18-26) he strongly emphasizes a corollary of this condition, namely that those who are not competent in demonstrative reasoning ought not to be permitted to hear allegorical interpretations.

The doctrine is worked out within the framework of a theory

[1] See L. Gauthier, *Théorie*, p. 104, for comments on Ibn Rushd's position.
[2] See *Manāhij*, 122-23 (in the extract translated below after *Faṣl*).

of intellectual classes, which is a development of Aristotelian logic.[1] The classification of types of reasoning in Aristotle's Organon was well known to the Muslim philosophers.[2] The three types that are relevant here are: (1) demonstrative reasoning, based on certain premisses, (2) dialectical reasoning, based on opinions that are generally accepted and seem probable to thoughtful people, and (3) rhetorical reasoning, based on opinions that are persuasive to ordinary people but will not stand up to criticism. Adopting this classification, the Muslims went a step further and listed the corresponding types of mind, according to their ability to understand and willingness to accept the types of reasoning.[3] Thus, a demonstrative man understands demonstrative reasoning and fully accepts no other; a dialectical man cannot understand demonstrative science (e.g. metaphysics), but is not satisfied with rhetorical reasoning; while a rhetorical man cannot understand demonstrative science and is satisfied with rhetorical reasoning.

A scheme such as this leads necessarily to certain principles for education, including religious instruction: people must be taught enough to convince them, but not more than they can understand. In Ibn Rushd's view, the *Qur'ān* itself provides the perfect model for religious instruction. In the first place, it contains many plain texts which state their meaning directly and can be understood by every level of intellect (pp. 14-15). But besides these it contains allegorical texts, using symbols and images of such a kind that what they symbolize, their inner meaning (*bāṭin*), can only be understood, and even noticed, by the demonstrative class (pp. 19, 24-25); while the dialectical and rhetorical classes can only understand them on the surface, in their apparent meaning (*ẓāhir*), but this is enough to satisfy their needs and ambitions (pp. 14-15, 24-25). (An elaborate and dry classification of types of text is given on pp. 19-20, but we need not go over the details here.)

At this point we may consider a criticism, which was levelled against the view that the *Qur'ān* contained a hidden *bāṭin* as well as a *ẓāhir*. Since the *ẓāhir* would be strictly untrue, yet would be the most that the people could understand, we should have to conclude that God instructed His Prophet to teach the people lies. Such a charge may be brought against Ibn Rushd's theory: indeed, in his *Commentary on Plato's Republic* (not for popular consumption) he explicitly equated the allegories in Scripture with the "noble lie" of Plato's guardians.[4] But he is in good company; the same could

[1] See L. Gauthier, *Théorie*, pp. 40ff.

[2] For references see notes 24 and 25 to the translation.

[3] For references see note 56 to the translation.

[4] The equation becomes clear from a comparison of I, xii, 6; II, xvi, 6; and II, xvi, 8. Cf. also *Tafsīr mā ba'd aṭ-ṭabī'a*, ed. M. Bouyges, 4 vols. (Beirut, 1938-51), pp. 42-43.

be said against all except a few literalists. Ghazālī had already formulated and answered the objection in *Iḥyā' 'ulūm ad-dīn.*[1] Perhaps this is why Ibn Rushd does not answer it directly. But it is not hard to see that his answer would be of the same kind as Ghazālī's: that the revelation of certain truths to everyone is harmful,[2] and Scripture followed the only wise and moral course in this matter.[3]

To return to the thread of the argument: Scripture provides the model which the learned should follow in their teaching. Ghazālī wrote of the Prophet, and certain saints and scholars, that "they are trained in the manners of Scripture (*yata'addabūna bi-ādāb ash-shar'*) and keep silent on the same points as it".[4] Ibn Rushd's attitude is the same, and he elaborates it in accordance with his philosophic principles. In the first two chapters he has more than once laid down the conditions which entitle a man to study philosophy and learn the demonstrative interpretations of Scripture: he must have a keen natural intelligence, a good moral character, and sufficient instruction in philosophy by a teacher. He now gives the rules for explaining Scripture to the dialectical and rhetorical classes. The general principle to be followed is that the inner meanings, being interpretations only discoverable and understandable by demonstrative reasoning, must not be revealed to the two lower classes more than can be helped. If persons of those classes chance to suspect that there is a deeper meaning to a text, they must be given an explanation that they can understand and that will satisfy them (p. 21). Detailed rules are given for dealing with such cases.[5] To disclose more than is necessary is repeatedly condemned as unbelief (pp. 16, 17, 21, 22, 23).

Two explicit reasons are given for this prohibition. One is that to teach allegorical interpretations to people who cannot understand them breaks down their religion, since it undermines their belief in the apparent meaning of Scripture and sets nothing in its place (p. 21). In a parable in the Platonic manner, Ibn Rushd compares this offence with turning people against sound medicine and destroying their confidence in all medicine (pp. 22-23). Ghazālī had insisted on this danger in many passages of his writings—though he is criticized by Ibn Rushd for not practising what he preached, and divulging hidden truths in popular writings (pp. 17, 21).

[1] 'Irāqī ed., I, pp. 173-78.

[2] See below, pp. 34-35, on the harm as conceived by Ibn Rushd.

[3] In *Fayṣal*, pp. 90-91, Ghazālī tries to make out a special case against the philosophers; but I find some confusion in his argument and this is not the place to analyse it.

[4] *Iḥyā'*, I, p. 173; cf. Ben Maymón, *Guide*, Part 1, Introduction, and comments of L. Strauss, *Persecution*, pp. 60 ff.

[5] See especially *Manāhij*, 124-27.

The second reason for the prohibition is that an interest in allegories by people who are unable to understand them properly gives rise to dissensions and strife in Islam, through the growth of sects each with a particular doctrine. For this development Ibn Rushd blames particularly the theologians, both Ash'arites and Mu'tazilites, who have broadcast their allegorical interpretations among the masses (pp. 23-24). Still worse, most of these interpretations are false and have been arrived at by unsound methods (pp. 22-23, 24). The theologians are incompetent, because they belong to the dialectical class.[1]

There is a third reason for Ibn Rushd's prohibition, which is not stated but can, I think, be inferred from the total situation in which *Faṣl al-maqāl* appeared. This is the fact that philosophy was so deeply suspected and opposed by the Andalusian public that it could not hope to survive if it came out with public teaching about Scripture. Thus Chapter 3 may be regarded as Ibn Rushd's pledge to the learned classes to keep philosophy within limited circles. At the same time it contains a defensive counter-attack on the Ash'arites: since the philosophers cannot hope to teach their version of religion to the public, the next best thing was to prevent their rivals the theologians from teaching theirs.

Ibn Rushd's theory of religious instruction is no doubt open to the moral criticism that it encourages in teachers a lack of frankness, a spirit of secretiveness and duplicity.[2] We should be careful how we formulate such a criticism. The mere refusal to teach unprepared students is based on common sense educational reasons, which are as valid today as they have ever been. On this point Ibn Rushd was part of an immensely weighty philosophic tradition; from his predecessors Plato, Aristotle, the later Greek thinkers, Fārābī, Ibn Sīnā, Ibn Bājja and his contemporary Ibn Ṭufayl, he would learn one thing, not to teach philosophy to people who are not prepared for it. From his religious heritage he could pick up many hints to the same effect: from the *Qur'ān*, the Bible, and above all from his great predecessor and antagonist Ghazālī, whose works abound in warnings against "meat for babes".[3] We must make allowances, too, for the hostility to philosophy in his age, which made a certain caution in expression prudent for the philosopher and morally excusable.

Still, it is harder to excuse the deliberate evasiveness and even falsehood which he counsels in explaining Scripture to the un-

[1] The identification is made clear from the general argument of *Faṣl* and from statements in *Manāhij*, e.g. 56-57.

[2] Or triplicity, since there are three interpretations: e.g. 16, on the verses apparently relating God to space.

[3] See n. 142 to the translation for references to philosophic and religious antecedents.

learned: for example, *Qur'ān*, iii, 5, which speaks of "those who are well grounded in science", must be punctuated in one way in scientific writings and discussions (p. 10) and differently in public (p. 16). Such tactics are not acceptable to modern moral ideas, and the best that can be said for them is that here too Ibn Rushd had the authority of a long philosophic and religious tradition, including Ghazālī.[1]

He might be criticized further by modern opinion for holding an undemocratic view of higher education and wishing to limit it to a privileged élite (*al-khawāṣṣ*). Here once more he might convincingly plead educational necessity, and a very strong aristocratic tradition in philosophy. And we are not on sure ground as critics. It can easily be argued that we have gone too far in opening higher education of all kinds to the people, with too little regard for the necessity of adequate preparation. Ibn Rushd in the modern world might well be displeased with many of the products of our universities, classing them as dialecticians, sophists and rhetoricians.

Towards the end of *Faṣl* Ibn Rushd proposes the remedy for the ill caused by the theologians.

> "So whoever wishes to remove this heresy from religion should direct his attention to the precious Book, and glean from it the indications present [in it] concerning everything in turn that it obliges us to believe, and exercise his judgement in looking at its apparent meaning as well as he is able, without interpreting any of it allegorically, except where the allegorical meaning is apparent in itself, i.e. commonly apparent to everyone" (p. 25).

He announces his intention to achieve this object (p. 25). At the beginning of *Manāhij* he refers to *Faṣl* and gives us to understand that the work which follows is to carry out the proposed object. "In this book I think fit to inquire into the apparent meaning of the dogmas", following the intention of the Prophet.[2] Thus the link between the two books is clear. But the announcements lead us to expect a work of popular dogmatics, whereas in fact *Manāhij* turns out to be something different, a handbook of instruction for teachers of popular religion.[3] It discusses various theories and interpretations, and goes well beyond what Ibn Rushd thought fit for the masses to hear.

I have not considered it essential to publish *Manāhij* together with *Faṣl*. The two books differ in their subjects, in the manner

[1] E.g. in *Mīzān al-'amal*, ed. Kurdī (Cairo, 1910), pp. 212-16. Cf. Ben Maymōn, *Guide*, Part I, Introduction, and L. Strauss, *Persecution*, ch. 3.

[2] *Manāhij*, 27.

[3] Cf. Ghazālī's *Kitāb al-iqtiṣād fīl-i'tiqād*.

explained: *Faṣl* is a legal inquiry about philosophy, *Manāhij* is a work on dogmatic education. And although the latter illustrates many of the ideas of the former, *Faṣl* was written as a self-contained work and can stand alone.

GENERAL QUESTIONS

Such are the broad outlines of the argument of *Faṣl*. Some large questions may now be discussed concerning the treatise as a whole.

Does it present its author's true philosophic beliefs? This question must arise about all the works of any philosopher who believes in esoteric and exoteric writing. Without going into the whole tricky problem of criticism concerning such authors, we can safely assume on the basis of *Faṣl* and other works that Ibn Rushd believed strongly in the distinction and its necessity for philosophers, including himself. The first question to ask is therefore, In which category does *Faṣl* belong? The answer is given in the last paragraph of Chapter 2 (p. 18): "If it were not for the publicity given to the matter and to these questions which we have discussed, we should not have permitted ourselves to write a single word on the subject; and we should not have had to make excuses for doing so to the interpretative scholars, because the proper place to discuss these questions is in demonstrative books." Thus it is clear that *Faṣl* is an exoteric work about a normally esoteric subject.

Some clue to Ibn Rushd's policy in such a case is given in a passage of *Tahāfut at-tahāfut* which, like *Faṣl*, is designed to meet a challenge on topics which the author would not normally have discussed in a public work.[1] After mentioning his normal prohibition of public teaching on the question of God's knowledge, he brings in the familiar medical analogy of food and poison, which are relative to the condition of their consumers.

> "But when the wicked and ignorant transgress and bring poison to the man for whom it is really poison, as if it were nourishment, then there is need of a physician who through his science will exert himself to heal that man, and for this reason we have allowed ourselves to discuss this problem in such a book as this, and in any other case we should not regard this as permissible to us . . . And since it is impossible to avoid the discussion of this problem, let us treat it in such a way as is possible in this place for those who do not possess the preparation and mental training needed before entering upon speculation about it."[2]

[1] *Tahāfut at-tahāfut*, pp. 358, 588.

[2] p. 358, Eng. tr. S. Van den Bergh, *Averroes' Tahafut al-tahafut* (Oxford, 1954), I, p. 216. See also his notes, p. 215.2 and p. 216.1 and 2.

The passage seems to imply, in the first place, that Ibn Rushd's policy is to treat such subjects to the least extent and as briefly as possible. This would be in line with his recommendations in *Manāhij*[1] for speaking about allegorical passages of Scripture to unqualified people who suspect a deeper meaning: the philosopher should not reveal more than he can help. In the second place, it is implied that what is normally poison for the lower classes (demonstrative truth) can be used for the cure of their sick minds.[2]

When we examine the actual contents of *Tahāfut* we do not find them brief, but this may be due to the amount of ground that has to be covered. And, on the whole, his opinions here agree with those of his "demonstrative books", the summaries and commentaries on Aristotle.

Faṣl is brief and, as was said above, only deals with philosophic questions to the minimum extent necessary to establish the legal conclusions of the treatise. In its legal aspect the work has no need for reserve, but on explosive philosophic issues, such as the future life, it says as little as possible. I have not found in it any expression of views which actually contradict Ibn Rushd's "demonstrative" views.

Finally, given the problem as it presented itself, the answer is probably the only one possible. Ibn Rushd has fulfilled the requirements of a solution as well as he could within the limits set by his own convictions, and not abandoned those convictions. It must be concluded, then, that in *Faṣl* Ibn Rushd is presenting his true beliefs on philosophic matters, but exercising caution in discussing them.

Is he presenting his true beliefs on religion? The work shows him as a believing Muslim, but was he really such? This is a question which can hardly be answered on the basis of *Faṣl* alone. Here his starting-point is the *shar'*, so that by its very nature *Faṣl* accepts the *shar'*.[3] The impression made by the work is in my opinion one of sincerity. I think Ibn Rushd regarded himself as a Muslim, and really felt "the utmost sorrow and pain" at the misunderstandings that had arisen between the two "milk-sisters", religion and philosophy (pp. 25-26).

This impression is confirmed by a report about Ibn Rushd at the time of his trial and condemnation in 591 (1194/5). One of his biographers, Anṣārī, records the philosopher's feelings at that time in the following sentence: " 'The worst thing that happened to me

[1] 125-26.

[2] It is not implied by Ibn Rushd's statements that falsehood would be a cure for them. If we wish to press the implications we may infer that falsehood is their normal food; but on this view see above, pp. 33-34. For the medical simile cf. Ghazālī, *Iḥyā'*, I, pp. 167-68.

[3] See above, pp. 25-26, for the answer to a problem that arises at this point.

in my afflictions was when I and my son 'Abdallāh entered a mosque in Córdoba at the time of the evening prayer, and some of the lowest of the common people made a commotion against us and ejected us from it.' "[1] On matters of sincerity and motivation it is hard to satisfy the sceptic. But perhaps the crucial test is whether in his *philosophic* works Ibn Rushd has diverged from his master Aristotle in ways which can only be explained by his Islamic convictions; for in those works he would have no motive of prudence or persuasion to make concessions to Islam. This question has been acutely posed by Allard in relation to Ibn Rushd's views on the creation of the world.[2] Allard concludes that there are real divergences between Aristotle and Ibn Rushd in this question, and that they can only be explained by the supposition that as a Muslim he could not ignore the *Qur'anic* ideas of creation.[3]

What is the originality of *Faṣl*? As I said before, I believe it is the only book in medieval Islam which attempts a direct answer to its particular problem, the harmony of Sunnite Islam with Greco-Arabic philosophy. Many of the ideas used by Ibn Rushd in the solution are drawn from his predecessors, particularly Aristotle, Fārābī and Ghazālī; the notes to the translation will show his debts in detail. But Ibn Rushd is a master of intellectual alchemy, that typically Islamic art of blending ideas from different sources into a harmonious whole; and there is no doubt that in *Faṣl* the whole is something new and original.

What permanent value does *Faṣl* possess? Such a question may be understood in various ways and receive various answers. I can only offer a few opinions, in the hope that they will stimulate reflection in the minds of scholars.

It is tempting to say that Chapter 1 is a classic, Chapter 2 an Islamic classic, and Chapter 3 only a mediaeval Islamic classic. Such a judgement suggests the breadth of interest of each part, but it is too simple, ignoring the organic relations of the parts. Chapter 1 sets the problem in terms of Islamic religion and mediaeval philosophy. And it hardly begins to face the difficulties of an answer: this is done in Chapter 2. Perhaps these two chapters together may be considered a permanent classic of Islamic thought, while Chapter 3 is a product of a vanished mediaeval world. There is some truth in this; but we must not forget the mediaeval assumptions of the first two chapters about religion and philosophy,

[1] In E. Renan, *Averroès*, p. 439.

[2] "Le rationalisme d'Averroes d'après une étude sur la création": see especially pp. 20-27.

[3] *Ibid.*, pp. 53-55. Allard's study is mainly but not entirely based on *Tahāfut at-tahāfut*, which is not completely "demonstrative" as explained above. Still, on creation I believe its doctrine does not differ from anything held in the summaries and commentaries.

or the modern interest of the last in connection with religious education.

The fact is that we must consider any work first of all in terms of its time and environment, but that does not prevent it having a permanent value. If a work answers its own problem in a way that is unique yet inevitable, then it is a classic, of enduring interest not only to historians of thought but to all who concern themselves with similar problems in the setting of their own times. This is what *Faṣl* does, so that in spite of some archaic features it speaks to us directly in a language we can understand and appreciate.

The work in Arabic is elegant in a manner that no translation can reproduce. But it also contains a quality of spirit which appears in any language: a passionate intelligence which knows its goal and concentrates upon it. Here we meet an intensity of debate which almost summons up the missing opponents in Seville and Córdoba, with giant Abū Ḥāmid standing behind.

The Fate of the Work

No immediate reaction to *Faṣl* is recorded. Ibn Rushd continued to enjoy high posts under Abū Ya'qūb and his successor Abū Yūsuf (580-95 = 1184-1198/9), until the persecution of the philosophers and ban on philosophy carried out by the latter in 593 (1196/7).[1] Leaving aside the trivial causes suggested by some authors for the disgrace of Ibn Rushd, we are presented with enough evidence that the real cause was his philosophic activities. His condemnation was part of a general suppression of philosophy by the prince. Did *Faṣl* contribute anything to the annoyance of the conservative forces which brought about his exile? There is good reason to believe that it did. Anṣārī mentions among the offences of Ibn Rushd that "he sought to reconcile religion and philosophy (*al-jam' bayn ash-sharī'a wal-falsafa*)",[2] a phrase which recalls the title and subject of *Faṣl*. Elsewhere he says of the philosophers: "For they agree with the people in outward appearances (*fī ẓāhirihim*), in their dress and speech, but disagree with them in their inner ways (*bi-bāṭinihim*) and their error and calumny."[3] In a late work, the *Great Commentary* (*Tafsīr*) *on Aristotle's Metaphysics*, written around 586 (1190),[4] we find Ibn Rushd still attacking the Ash'arites in the same way as in *Faṣl* and *Manāhij*.[5]

After the philosopher's death, *Faṣl* made no great stir, but continued to be read by a few Andalusian scholars in the thirteenth

[1] This date is given by Ibn Khaldūn, *Histoire des Berbères*, II, p. 214.
[2] In E. Renan, *Averroès*, p. 444.
[3] *Ibid.*, p. 441.
[4] Date conjectured by Alonso, pp. 96-97.
[5] *Tafsīr mā ba'd aṭ-ṭabī'a*, pp. 43, 44-47, 1135-36.

and fourteenth centuries. The two Arabic manuscripts which survive were made in Andalus and are dated 633 (1234/5) and 724 (1323/4).[1] A Hebrew translation was made in the late thirteenth or early fourteenth century, and four manuscripts of it have survived in libraries of Western Europe.[2] *Faṣl* was apparently not translated into Latin, for it does not appear in the Latin corpus of Averroes. Whether it had any indirect influence on the ideas of the Latin Averroists is a question beyond my competence to answer. The appendix, "*Ḍamīma*", on God's knowledge of particulars, was put into Latin by Raymund Martin in the thirteenth century, and his translation has been edited and published again in our time.[3]

In the Muslim world at large *Faṣl* fell out of circulation. Ibn Khaldūn in the late fourteenth century made no reference to it in his critical account of the *falāsifa*,[4] though he was generally acquainted with Ibn Rushd's works and wrote summaries of (*lakhkhaṣa*) many of them.[5] Nor did any other scholar refer to it, and only the title remained on record in lists of Ibn Rushd's works.[6] *Manāhij* on the other hand was more widely known, having survived in one manuscript in Spain, two in Istanbul and two in Cairo; and it was criticized by the Hanbalite theologian Ibn Taymīya (d. 728 = 1327/8).[7]

Faṣl remained unknown in East and West until the middle of the nineteenth century; when Munk and Renan made their studies of Ibn Rushd they were not aware of it.[8] It was brought to light once more by M. J. Müller, who edited the Arabic text in 1859 from a single manuscript at the Escurial Library.[9] Since then other editions have been published by an anonymous scholar in Cairo, by L. Gauthier in Algiers, and by myself.[10]

1 For details see Hourani, Introduction, pp. 7-9.

2 For details see N. Golb, "The Hebrew translation of Averroes' *Faṣl al-maqāl*", *Proceedings of the American Academy for Jewish Research*, **25** (1956), pp. 91-113, and **26** (1957), pp. 41-64.

3 By M. Asín Palacios in *Homenaje*; reproduced by Alonso, pp. 357-65.

4 *Prolégomènes*, III, pp. 209-20. Ibn Khaldūn does follow Ibn Rushd's scheme of intellectual classes; see M. Mahdī, *Ibn Khaldūn's philosophy of history* (London, 1957), pp. 92-97. He could have obtained this from *Manāhij*. On the other hand he may have read *Faṣl* but preferred not to mention it.

5 Maqqari, *Nafḥ aṭ-ṭīb* (Cairo, 1949), VIII, p. 286.

6 See Hourani, note A.

7 *K. al-jamʿ bayn al-ʿaql wan-naql*, extracts in *Falsafat Ibn Rushd* (Cairo, no date, Raḥmānīya Press), pp. 128-40.

8 S. Munk, *Mélanges de philosophie juive et arabe* (Paris, 1859); E. Renan, *Averroès et l'Averroïsme*, 1st ed. (Paris, 1852).

9 *Philosophie und Theologie von Averroes* (Munich, 1859), based on MS. 632 in H. Derenbourg, *Les manuscrits arabes de l'Escurial* (Paris, 1884), I, p. 437.

10 Main editions: *Falsafat Ibn Rushd* (Cairo, no date, Raḥmānīya Press), which follows Müller closely; L. Gauthier, *Ibn Rochd* (*Averroès*): *Traité décisif* (Algiers, 1942 and 1948). G. F. Hourani, *Ibn Rushd* (*Averroes*): *Kitāb faṣl al-maqāl* (Leiden, 1959). For further details see Hourani.

Translations into modern languages have appeared in the following works:

German: M. J. Müller, *Philosophie und Theologie von Averroes* (Munich, 1875).

French: L. Gauthier, three versions:

1st, "Accord de la religion et de la philosophie, traduit et annoté", in *Recueil de mémoires et de textes, publiés en l'honneur du XIVème Congrès des Orientalistes* (Algiers, 1905).

2nd, *Ibn Rochd (Averroès): Traité décisif (Façl el-maqâl) sur l'accord de la religion et de la philosophie* (Algiers, 1942), opposite the text.

3rd, entitled as the second (Algiers, 1948), with minor corrections.

English: M. Jamil ur-Rehman, *The philosophy and theology of Averroes* (Baroda, 1921), inaccurate.

Spanish: M. Alonso, *Teología de Averroes* (Madrid-Granada, 1947).

Turkish: Nevzad Ayasbeyoglu, *Ibn Rüşd'un felsefesi* (Ankara, 1955).

All the editions and translations contain *Ḍamīma*, and all except those of Gauthier contain *Manāhij* as well.

These works, together with the many references to *Faṣl* in books and articles discussing Ibn Rushd's attitude to religion and philosophy,[1] testify to the interest shown by orientalists in the treatise. But it cannot be said that much interest in it has yet been felt by the wider public that concerns itself with the problems and history of religion and philosophy.

The Present Translation

The minimum justification for this new translation of *Faṣl al-maqāl* is twofold. Firstly, it is based on a new text, which I have been able to provide in my Arabic edition (Leiden: E. J. Brill, 1959) principally owing to the use of a second manuscript, known but unused in previous editions. This is MS. 5013 of the Biblioteca Nacional of Madrid. It is older than the Escurial manuscript, being dated 633 (1234/5), i.e. between 55 and 60 years after *Faṣl* was written. From a study of it many new readings have emerged, as a result of which the treatise appears more meaningful and clearer than before. I have also profited from the mediaeval Hebrew translation, with the generous assistance of its editor, Dr. Norman Golb.[2] Secondly, up to the present there has not been a satisfactory translation in English. In addition to these reasons, I hope that the introduction, translation, summaries and notes will contribute at numerous points to the understanding of the work.

[1] See above, p. 18, n. 6, for a list of the most important discussions.

[2] See Hourani, Introduction, for more details. Hebrew edition by N. Golb in *Proc. Amer. Acad. for Jewish Research*, **25** (1956) and **26** (1957).

The principles of my translation have been those of most others: to reproduce the author's meaning as exactly as possible and in good English. Where these two requirements conflict I have generally given priority to the former. But translation is always a compromise and one person's judgement will not always agree with another's. As far as I have been able I have used a constant translation for every technical or semi-technical word, to assist the reader to follow the philosopher's reasoning in single passages and to compare what he says on the same subject in different passages. Some of these renderings are justified in the notes, on the first occasion of their use. In the few cases where uniformity has proved impossible, I have translated with one of two words according to the context, and explained my practice in the notes. The paragraphs into which the translation is divided follow those of my Arabic edition, except in a few places where the translation contains an improved division.

1 # THE DECISIVE TREATISE, DETERMINING THE NATURE OF THE CONNECTION BETWEEN RELIGION AND PHILOSOPHY[1]

[What is the attitude of the Law to philosophy?]

Thus spoke the lawyer, *imām*, judge, and unique scholar, Abul Walīd Muḥammad Ibn Aḥmad Ibn Rushd:

6 Praise be to God with all due praise, and a prayer for Muḥammad His chosen servant and apostle. The purpose of this treatise[2] is to examine, from the standpoint of the study of the Law,[3] whether the study of philosophy and logic[4] is allowed by the Law,[5] or prohibited, or commanded—either by way of recommendation or as obligatory.[6]

[Chapter One]

[THE LAW MAKES PHILOSOPHIC STUDIES OBLIGATORY]

[If teleological study of the world is philosophy, and if the Law commands such a study, then the Law commands philosophy.][7]

10 We say: If the activity of 'philosophy' is nothing more than study of existing beings[8] and reflection on them as indications[9] of the Artisan,[10] i.e. inasmuch as they are products of art (for beings only indicate the Artisan through our knowledge of the art in them, and the more perfect this knowledge is, the more perfect the knowledge of the Artisan becomes),[11] and if the Law has encouraged and urged reflection on beings, then it is clear that what this name signifies is either obligatory or recommended by the Law.

[The Law commands such a study.][12]

15 That the Law summons to reflection on beings, and the pursuit of knowledge about them, by the intellect is clear from several

verses of the Book of God, Blessed and Exalted, such as the saying 2
of the Exalted, 'Reflect, you have vision:'[13] this is textual authority for the obligation[14] to use intellectual reasoning, or a combination of intellectual and legal reasoning.[15] Another example is His saying, 'Have they not studied the kingdom of the heavens and the earth, and whatever things God has created?':[16] this is a text urging the study of the totality of beings. Again, God the Exalted has taught that one of those whom He singularly honoured by this knowledge was Abraham, peace on him, for the Exalted said, 'So we made Abraham see the kingdom of the heavens and the earth, that he might be' [and so on to the end of the verse].[17] The Exalted also said, 'Do they not observe the camels, how they have been created, and the sky, how it has been raised up?',[18] and He said, 'and they give thought to the creation of the heavens and the earth',[19] and so on in countless other verses.[20]

> [This study must be conducted in the best manner, by demonstrative reasoning.][21]

Since it has now been established that the Law has rendered obligatory the study of beings by the intellect, and reflection on them, and since reflection is nothing more than inference and drawing out of the unknown from the known, and since this is reasoning[22] or at any rate done by reasoning, therefore we are under an obligation to carry on our study of beings by intellectual reasoning. It is further evident that this manner of study, to which the Law summons and urges, is the most perfect kind of study using the most perfect kind of reasoning;[23] and this is the kind called 'demonstration'.[24]

> [To master this instrument the religious thinker must make a preliminary study of logic, just as the lawyer must study legal reasoning. This is no more heretical in the one case than in the other. And logic must be learned from the ancient masters, regardless of the fact that they were not Muslims.]

The Law, then, has urged us to have demonstrative knowledge of God the Exalted and all the beings of His creation. But it is preferable and even necessary for anyone, who wants to understand God the Exalted and the other beings demonstratively, to have first understood the kinds of demonstration and their conditions [of validity], and in what respects demonstrative reasoning differs from dialectical, rhetorical and fallacious reasoning.[25] But this is not possible unless he has previously learned what reasoning as such is, and how many kinds it has, and which of them are valid

and which invalid.[26] This in turn is not possible unless he has previously learned the parts of reasoning, of which it is composed, i.e. the premisses and their kinds.[27] Therefore he who believes in the Law, and obeys its command to study beings, ought prior to his study to gain a knowledge of these things, which have the same
3 place in theoretical studies as instruments have in practical activities.[28]

For just as the lawyer infers from the Divine command to him to acquire knowledge of the legal categories[29] that he is under obligation to know the various kinds of legal syllogisms,[30] and which are valid and which invalid,[31] in the same way he who would know [God][32] ought to infer from the command to study beings that he is under obligation to acquire a knowledge of intellectual reasoning and its kinds. Indeed it is more fitting for him to do so, for if the lawyer infers from the saying of the Exalted, 'Reflect, you who have vision', the obligation to acquire a knowledge of legal reasoning, how much more fitting and proper that he who would know God should infer from it the obligation to acquire a knowledge of intellectual reasoning!

It cannot be objected: 'This kind of study of intellectual reasoning is a heretical innovation since it did not exist among the first believers.' For the study of legal reasoning and its kinds is also something which has been discovered since the first believers, yet it is not considered to be a heretical innovation. So the objector should believe the same about the study of intellectual reasoning.[33] (For this there is a reason, which it is not the place to mention here.) But most ⟨masters⟩ of this religion support intellectual reasoning, except a small group of gross literalists, who can be refuted by [sacred] texts.[34]

Since it has now been established that there is an obligation of the Law to study intellectual reasoning and its kinds, just as there is an obligation to study legal reasoning, it is clear that, if none of our predecessors had formerly examined intellectual reasoning and its kinds, we should be obliged to undertake such an examination from the beginning, and that each succeeding scholar would have to seek help in that task from his predecessor in order that knowledge of the subject might be completed.[35] For it is difficult or impossible for one man to find out by himself and from the beginning all that he needs of that subject, as it is difficult for one man to discover all the knowledge that he needs of the kinds of legal reasoning; indeed this is even truer of knowledge of intellectual reasoning.[36]

But if someone other than ourselves has already examined that subject, it is clear that we ought to seek help towards our goal from what has been said by such a predecessor on the subject, regardless

of whether this other one shares our religion or not.[37] For when a valid sacrifice[38] is performed with a certain instrument, no account 4
is taken, in judging the validity of the sacrifice, of whether the instrument belongs to one who shares our religion or to one who does not, so long as it fulfils the conditions for validity. By 'those who do not share our religion' I refer to those ancients who studied these matters before Islam. So if such is the case, and everything that is required in the study of the subject of intellectual syllogisms has already been examined in the most perfect manner by the ancients, presumably we ought to lay hands on their books in order to study what they said about that subject; and if it is all correct we should accept it from them, while if there is anything incorrect in it, we should draw attention to that.[39]

> [After logic we must proceed to philosophy proper. Here too we have to learn from our predecessors, just as in mathematics and law. Thus it is wrong to forbid the study of ancient philosophy. Harm from it is accidental, like harm from taking medicine, drinking water, or studying law.]

When we have finished with this sort of study and acquired the instruments by whose aid we are able to reflect on beings and the indications of art in them (for he who does not understand the art does not understand the product of art, and he who does not understand the product of art does not understand the Artisan), then we ought to begin the examination of beings in the order and manner we have learned from the art of demonstrative syllogisms.[40]

And again it is clear that in the study of beings this aim can be fulfilled by us perfectly only through successive examinations of them by one man after another,[41] the later ones seeking the help of the earlier in that task, on the model of what has happened in the mathematical sciences. For if we suppose that the art of geometry did not exist in this age of ours, and likewise the art of astronomy, and a single person wanted to ascertain by himself the sizes of the heavenly bodies, their shapes, and their distances from each other, that would not be possible for him—e.g. to know the proportion of the sun to the earth or other facts about the sizes of the stars—even though he were the most intelligent of men by nature, unless by a revelation or something resembling revelation.[42] Indeed if he were told that the sun is about 150 or 160 times[43] as great as the earth, he would think this statement madness on the part of the speaker, although this is a fact which has been demonstrated in astronomy so surely that no one who has mastered that science doubts it.

But what calls even more strongly for comparison with the art

5 of mathematics in this respect is the art of the principles of law; and the study of law itself was completed only over a long period of time. And if someone today wanted to find out by himself all the arguments which have been discovered by the theorists of the legal schools on controversial questions, about which debate has taken place between them in most countries of Islam (except the West),[44] he would deserve to be ridiculed, because such a task is impossible for him, apart from the fact that the work has been done already. Moreover, this is a situation that is self-evident not in the scientific arts alone but also in the practical arts; for there is not one of them which a single man can construct by himself. Then how can he do it with the art of arts, philosophy? If this is so, then whenever we find in the works of our predecessors of former nations a theory about beings and a reflection on them conforming to what the conditions of demonstration require, we ought to study what they said about the matter and what they affirmed in their books. And we should accept from them gladly and gratefully whatever in these books accords with the truth, and draw attention to and warn against what does not accord with the truth, at the same time excusing them.[45]

From this it is evident that the study of the books of the ancients is obligatory by Law, since their aim and purpose in their books is just the purpose to which the Law has urged us, and that whoever forbids the study of them to anyone who is fit to study them, i.e. anyone who unites two qualities, (1) natural intelligence and (2) religious integrity and moral virtue,[46] is blocking people from the door by which the Law summons them to knowledge of God, the door of theoretical study which leads to the truest knowledge of Him; and such an act is the extreme of ignorance and estrangement from God the Exalted.[47]

And if someone errs or stumbles in the study of these books owing to a deficiency in his natural capacity, or bad organization of his study of them, or being dominated by his passions, or not finding a teacher to guide him to an understanding of their contents, or a combination of all or more than one of these causes,[48] it does
6 not follow that one should forbid them to anyone who is qualified to study them. For this manner of harm which arises owing to them is something that is attached to them by accident, not by essence; and when a thing is beneficial by its nature and essence, it ought not to be shunned because of something harmful contained in it by accident.[49] This was the thought of the Prophet, peace on him, on the occasion when he ordered a man to give his brother honey to drink for his diarrhoea, and the diarrhoea increased after he had given him the honey: when the man complained to him about it, he said, 'God spoke the truth; it was your brother's stomach that

lied.'[50] We can even say that a man who prevents a qualified person from studying books of philosophy, because some of the most vicious people may be thought to have gone astray through their study of them,[51] is like a man who prevents a thirsty person from drinking cool, fresh water until he dies of thirst, because some people have choked to death on it. For death from water by choking is an accidental matter, but death by thirst is essential and necessary.

Moreover, this accidental effect of this art is a thing which may also occur accidentally from the other arts. To how many lawyers has law been a cause of lack of piety and immersion in this world! Indeed we find most lawyers in this state, although their art by its essence calls for nothing but practical virtue. Thus it is not strange if the same thing that occurs accidentally in the art which calls for practical virtue should occur accidentally in the art which calls for intellectual virtue.[52]

[For every Muslim the Law has provided a way to truth suitable to his nature, through demonstrative, dialectical or rhetorical methods.][53]

Since all this is now established, and since we, the Muslim community, hold that this divine religion of ours is true,[54] and that it is this religion which incites and summons us to the happiness that consists in the knowledge of God, Mighty and Majestic, and of His creation, that [end][55] is appointed for every Muslim by the method of assent which his temperament and nature require. For the natures of men are on different levels with respect to [their paths to] assent. One of them comes to assent through demonstration; another comes to assent through dialectical arguments, just as firmly as the demonstrative man through demonstration, since his nature does not contain any greater capacity; while another comes to assent through rhetorical arguments, again just as firmly as the demonstrative man through demonstrative arguments.[56]

Thus since this divine religion of ours has summoned people by 7
these three methods, assent to it has extended to everyone, except him who stubbornly denies it with his tongue or him for whom no method of summons to God the Exalted has been appointed in religion owing to his own neglect of such matters.[57] It was for this purpose that the Prophet, peace on him, was sent with a special mission to 'the white man[58] and the black man' alike; I mean because his religion embraces all the methods of summons to God the Exalted. This is clearly expressed in the saying of God the Exalted, 'Summon to the way of your Lord by wisdom and by good preaching, and debate with them in the most effective manner'.[59]

[Chapter Two]

[PHILOSOPHY CONTAINS NOTHING OPPOSED TO ISLAM]

[Demonstrative truth and scriptural truth cannot conflict.][60]

Now since this religion is true and summons to the study which leads to knowledge of the Truth, we the Muslim community know definitely that demonstrative study does not lead to [conclusions] conflicting with what Scripture has given us; for truth does not oppose truth but accords with it and bears witness to it.

[If the apparent meaning of Scripture conflicts with demonstrative conclusions it must be interpreted allegorically, i.e. metaphorically.]

This being so, whenever demonstrative study leads to any manner of knowledge about any being, that being is inevitably either unmentioned or mentioned in Scripture. If it is unmentioned there is no contradiction, and it is in the same case as an act whose category is unmentioned, so that the lawyer has to infer it by reasoning from Scripture.[61] If Scripture speaks about it, the apparent meaning of the words inevitably either accords or conflicts with the conclusions of demonstration about it. If this [apparent meaning] accords there is no argument. If it conflicts there is a call for allegorical interpretation of it. The meaning of 'allegorical interpretation' is: extension of the significance of an expression from real to metaphorical significance, without forsaking therein the standard metaphorical practices of Arabic, such as calling a thing by the name of something resembling it or a cause or consequence or accompaniment of it, or other things such as are enumerated in accounts of the kinds of metaphorical speech.[62]

[If the lawyer can do this, the religious thinker certainly can. Indeed these allegorical interpretations always receive confirmation from the apparent meaning of other passages of Scripture.]

Now if the lawyer does this in many decisions of religious law, with how much more right is it done by the possessor of demonstrative knowledge![63] For the lawyer has at his disposition only reasoning based on opinion,[64] while he who would know [God] ⟨has at his disposition⟩ reasoning based on certainty. So we affirm definitely that whenever the conclusion of a demonstration is in conflict with the apparent meaning of Scripture, that apparent **8**
meaning admits of allegorical interpretation according to the rules for such interpretation in Arabic. This proposition is questioned by no Muslim and doubted by no believer.[65] But its certainty is immensely increased for those who have had close dealings with this idea and put it to the test, and made it their aim to reconcile the assertions of intellect and tradition.[66] Indeed we may say that whenever a statement in Scripture conflicts in its apparent meaning with a conclusion of demonstration, if Scripture is considered carefully, and the rest of its contents searched page by page, there will invariably be found among the expressions of Scripture something which in its apparent meaning bears witness to that allegorical interpretation[67] or comes close to bearing witness.

> [All Muslims accept the principle of allegorical interpretation; they only disagree about the extent of its application.]

In the light of this idea the Muslims are unanimous[68] in holding that it is not obligatory either to take all the expressions of Scripture in their apparent meaning or to extend them all from their apparent meaning by allegorical interpretation. They disagree [only] over which of them should and which should not be so interpreted: the Ash'arites for instance give an allegorical interpretation[69] to the verse about God's directing Himself[70] and the Tradition about His descent,[71] while the Hanbalites take them in their apparent meaning.[72]

> [The double meaning has been given to suit people's diverse intelligence. The apparent contradictions are meant to stimulate the learned to deeper study.]

The reason why we have received a Scripture with both an apparent and an inner meaning lies in the diversity of people's natural capacities and the difference of their innate dispositions with regard to assent. The reason why we have received in Scripture texts whose apparent meanings contradict each other is in order to draw the attention of those who are well grounded in science to the interpretation which reconciles them.[73] This is the idea referred to in the words received from the Exalted, 'He it is who has sent down to you the Book, containing certain verses clear and definite' [and so on] down to the words 'those who are well grounded in science'.[74]

> [In interpreting texts allegorically we must never violate Islamic consensus, when it is certain. But to establish it with certainty with regard to theoretical texts is impossible, because there have always been scholars who would not divulge their interpretation of such texts.]

It may be objected: 'There are some things in Scripture which the Muslims have unanimously agreed to take in their apparent meaning, others [which they have agreed] to interpret allegorically, and others about which they have disagreed;[75] is it permissible, then, that demonstration should lead to interpreting allegorically what they have agreed to take in its apparent meaning, or to taking in its apparent meaning what they have agreed to interpret allegorically?' We reply: If unanimous agreement is established by a method which is certain, such [a result] is not sound; but if [the existence of] agreement on those things is a matter of opinion, then it may be sound. This is why Abū Ḥāmid,[76] Abul-Ma'ālī,[77] and other leaders of thought said that no one should be definitely called an unbeliever for violating unanimity on a point of interpretation in matters like these.[78]

That unanimity on theoretical matters is never determined with certainty, as it can be on practical matters, may be shown to you
9 by the fact that it is not possible for unanimity to be determined on any question at any period unless that period is strictly limited by us, and all the scholars existing in that period are known to us (i.e. known as individuals and in their total number), and the doctrine of each of them on the question has been handed down to us on unassailable authority,[79] and, in addition to all this, unless we are sure that the scholars existing at the time were in agreement that there is not both an apparent and an inner meaning in Scripture, that knowledge of any question ought not to be kept secret from anyone, and that there is only one way for people to understand Scripture. But it is recorded in Tradition that many of the first believers used to hold that Scripture has both an apparent and an inner meaning, and that the inner meaning ought not to be learned by anyone who is not a man of learning in this field and who is incapable of understanding it. Thus, for example, Bukhārī reports a saying of 'Alī Ibn Abī Ṭālib, may God be pleased with him, 'Speak to people about what they know. Do you want God and His Prophet to be accused of lying?'[80] Other examples of the same kind are reported about a group of early believers.[81] So

how can it possibly be conceived that a unanimous agreement can have been handed down to us about a single theoretical question, when we know definitely that not a single period has been without scholars who held that there are things in Scripture whose true meaning should not be learned by all people?

The situation is different in practical matters: everyone holds that the truth about these should be disclosed to all people alike, and to establish the occurrence of unanimity about them we consider it sufficient that the question [at issue] should have been widely discussed and that no report of controversy about it should have been handed down to us.[82] This is enough to establish the occurrence of unanimity on matters of practice, but on matters of doctrine the case is different.

[Ghazālī's charge of unbelief against Fārābī and Ibn Sīnā, for asserting the world's eternity and God's ignorance of particulars and denying bodily resurrection, is only tentative, not definite.]

You may object: 'If we ought not to call a man an unbeliever for violating unanimity in cases of allegorical interpretation, because no unanimity is conceivable in such cases, what do you say about the Muslim philosophers, like Abū Naṣr[83] and Ibn Sīnā?[84] For Abū Ḥāmid called them both definitely unbelievers in the book of his known as *The disintegration*,[85] on three counts: their assertions of the pre-eternity of the world and that God the Exalted does not know particulars' (may He be Exalted far above that [ignorance]!), 'and their allegorical interpretation of the passages concerning **10**
the resurrection of bodies and states of existence in the next life.'

We answer: It is apparent from what he said on the subject that his calling them both unbelievers on these counts was not definite, since he made it clear in *The book of the distinction* that calling people unbelievers for violating unanimity can only be tentative.[86]

[Such a charge cannot be definite, because there has never been a consensus against allegorical interpretation. The *Qur'ān* itself indicates that it has inner meanings which it is the special function of the demonstrative class to understand.]

Moreover, it is evident from what we have said that a unanimous agreement cannot be established in questions of this kind, because of the reports that many of the early believers of the first generation, as well as others, have said that there are allegorical interpretations which ought not to be expressed except to those who are qualified to receive allegories. These are 'those who are well grounded in science'; for we prefer to place the stop after the words of God the Exalted 'and those who are well grounded in science', because if the scholars did not understand allegorical interpretation, there would be no superiority in their assent which would oblige them to a belief in Him not found among the unlearned.[87] God has described them as those who believe in Him, and this can only be taken to refer to the belief which is based on demonstration; and this [belief][88] only occurs together with the science of allegorical interpretation.[89] For the unlearned believers are those whose belief in Him is not based on demonstration; and if this belief which God has attributed to the scholars is peculiar to them, it must come through demonstration, and if it comes through demonstration it only occurs together with the science of allegorical interpretation.[90] For God the Exalted has informed us that those [verses] have [91] an allegorical interpretation which is the truth, and demonstration can only be of the truth. That being the case, it is not possible for general unanimity[92] to be established about allegorical interpretations, which God has made peculiar to scholars. This is self-evident to any fair-minded person.

> [Besides, Ghazālī was mistaken in ascribing to the Peripatetics the opinion that God does not know particulars. Their view is that His knowledge of both particulars and universals differs from ours, in being the cause, not an effect, of the object known. They even hold that God sends premonitions in dreams of particular events.][93]

In addition to all this we hold that Abū Ḥāmid was mistaken about the Peripatetic philosophers, in ascribing to them the assertion that God, Holy and Exalted, does not know particulars at all.[94] In reality they hold that God the Exalted knows them in a way which is not of the same kind as our way of knowing them. For our knowledge of them is an effect of the object known, originated when it comes into existence and changing when it changes; whereas Glorious God's Knowledge of existence is the opposite of this: it is the cause of the object known, which is existent being.
11 Thus to suppose the two kinds of knowledge similar to each other is to identify the essences and properties of opposite things, and that is the extreme of ignorance. And if the name of 'knowledge' is predicated of both originated and eternal knowledge, it is predicated by sheer homonymy, as many names are predicated of opposite things: e.g. *jalal* of great and small, *ṣarīm* of light and darkness.[95] Thus there exists no definition embracing both kinds of knowledge at once, as the theologians of our time imagine. We have devoted a separate essay to this question, impelled by one of our friends.[96]

But how can anyone imagine that the Peripatetics say that God the Glorious does not know particulars with His eternal Knowledge, when they hold that true visions[97] include premonitions of particular events due to occur in future time, and that this warning foreknowledge comes to people in their sleep from the eternal Knowledge which orders and rules the universe?[98] Moreover, it is not only particulars which they say God does not know in the manner in which we know them, but universals as well; for the universals known to us are also effects of the nature of existent being, while with His Knowledge the reverse is true. Thus the conclusion to which demonstration leads is that His Knowledge transcends qualification as 'universal' or 'particular'. Consequently there is no point in disputing about this question, i.e. whether to call them unbelievers or not.

> [On the question of the world, the ancient philosophers agree with the Ash'arites that it is originated and coeval with time. The Peripatetics only disagree with the Ash'arites and the Platonists in holding that past time is infinite. This difference is insufficient to justify a charge of unbelief.][99]

Concerning the question whether the world is pre-eternal or came into existence, the disagreement between the Ash'arite theologians and the ancient philosophers is in my view almost resolvable into a disagreement about naming, especially in the case of certain of the ancients. For they agree that there are three classes of beings: two extremes and one intermediate between the extremes. They agree also about naming the extremes; but they disagree about the intermediate class.

[1] One extreme is a being which is brought into existence from something other than itself and by something, i.e. by an efficient cause and from some matter; and it, i.e. its existence, is preceded by time. This is the status of bodies whose generation is apprehended by sense, e.g. the generation of water, air, earth, 12
animals, plants, and so on. All alike, ancients and Ash'arites, agree in naming this class of beings 'originated'. [2] The opposite extreme to this is a being which is not made from or by anything and not preceded by time; and here too all members of both schools agree in naming it 'pre-eternal'. This being is apprehended by demonstration; it is God, Blessed and Exalted, Who is the Maker,[100] Giver of being and Sustainer of the universe; may He be praised and His Power exalted!

[3] The class of being which is between these two extremes is that which is not made from anything and not preceded by time, but which is brought into existence by something, i.e. by an agent.

This is the world as a whole. Now they all agree on the presence of these three characters in the world. For the theologians admit that time does not precede it, or rather this is a necessary consequence for them since time according to them is something which accompanies motion and bodies. They also agree with the ancients in the view that future time is infinite and likewise future being. They only disagree about past time and past being: the theologians hold that it[101] is finite (this is the doctrine of Plato and his followers),[102] while Aristotle and his school hold that it is infinite, as is the case with future time.

Thus it is clear that [3] this last being bears a resemblance both to [1] the being which is really generated[103] and to [2] the pre-eternal Being. So those who are more impressed with its resemblance to the pre-eternal than its resemblance to the originated name it 'pre-eternal', while those who are more impressed with its resemblance to the originated name it 'originated'. But in truth it is neither really originated nor really pre-eternal, since the really originated is necessarily perishable and the really pre-eternal has no cause. Some—Plato and his followers—name it 'originated and coeval with time',[104] because time according to them is finite in the past.

Thus the doctrines about the world are not so very far apart from each other that some of them should be called irreligious
13 and others not. For this to happen, opinions must be divergent in the extreme, i.e. contraries such as the theologians suppose to exist on this question; i.e. [they hold] that the names 'pre-eternity' and 'coming into existence' as applied to the world as a whole are contraries. But it is now clear from what we have said that this is not the case.[105]

> [Anyhow, the apparent meaning of Scripture is that there was a being and time before God created the present being and time. Thus the theologians' interpretation is allegorical and does not command unanimous agreement.]

Over and above all this, these opinions[106] about the world do not conform to the apparent meaning of Scripture. For if the apparent meaning of Scripture is searched, it will be evident from the verses which give us information about the bringing into existence of the world that its form really is originated,[107] but that being itself and time extend continuously at both extremes, i.e. without interruption. Thus the words of God the Exalted, 'He it is Who created the heavens and the earth in six days, and His throne was on the water',[108] taken in their apparent meaning imply that there was a being before this present being, namely the throne and the water, and a time before this time, i.e. the one which is joined to the form of this being, namely the number of the movement of the celestial sphere. And the words of the Exalted, 'On the day when the earth shall be changed into other than earth, and the heavens as well,'[109] also in their apparent meaning imply that there will be a second being after this being. And the words of the Exalted 'Then He directed Himself towards the sky, and it was smoke',[110] in their apparent meaning imply that the heavens were created from something.

Thus the theologians too in their statements about the world do not conform to the apparent meaning of Scripture but interpret it allegorically. For it is not stated in Scripture that God was existing with absolutely nothing else: a text to this effect is nowhere to be found. Then how is it conceivable that the theologians' allegorical interpretation of these verses could meet with unanimous agreement, when the apparent meaning of Scripture which we have mentioned about the existence of the world has been accepted by a school of philosophers![111]

> [On such difficult questions, error committed by a qualified judge of his subject is excused by God, while error by an unqualified person is not excused.][112]

It seems that those who disagree on the interpretation of these difficult questions earn merit if they are in the right and will be excused [by God] if they are in error.[113] For assent to a thing as a result of an indication [of it] arising in the soul is something compulsory, not voluntary: i.e. it is not for us [to choose] not to assent or to assent, as it is to stand up or not to stand up.[114] And since free choice is a condition of obligation,[115] a man who assents to an error as a result of a consideration that has occurred to him is excused, if he is a scholar. This is why the Prophet, peace on him, 14
said, 'If the judge after exerting his mind makes a right decision, he will have a double reward; and if he makes a wrong decision he will [still] have a single reward.'[116] And what judge is more important than he who makes judgements about being, that it is thus or not thus? These judges are the scholars, specially chosen by God for [the task of] allegorical interpretation, and this error which is forgivable according to the Law is only such error as proceeds from scholars when they study the difficult matters which the Law obliges them to study.[117]

But error proceeding from any other class of people is sheer sin, equally whether it relates to theoretical or to practical matters. For just as the judge who is ignorant of the [Prophet's] way of life is not excused if he makes an error in judgement, so he who makes judgements about beings without having the proper qualifications for [such] judgements is not excused but is either a sinner or an unbeliever. And if he who would judge what is allowed and forbidden is required to combine in himself the qualifications for exercise of personal judgement, namely knowledge of the principles [of law] and knowledge of how to draw inferences from those principles by reasoning, how much more properly is he who would make judgements about beings required to be qualified, i.e. to know the primary intellectual principles and the way to draw inferences from them![118]

> [Texts of Scripture fall into three kinds with respect to the excusability of error. [1] Texts which must be taken in their apparent meaning by everyone. Since the meaning can be understood plainly by demonstrative, dialectical and rhetorical methods alike, no one is excused for the error of interpreting these texts allegorically. [2] Texts which must be taken in their apparent meaning by the lower classes and interpreted allegorically by the demonstrative class. It is inexcusable for the lower classes to interpret them allegorically or for the demonstrative class to take them in their apparent meaning. [3] Texts whose classification under the previous headings is uncertain. Error in this matter by the demonstrative class is excused.][119]

In general, error about Scripture is of two types:[120] either error which is excused to one who is a qualified student of that matter in which the error occurs (as the skilful doctor is excused if he commits an error in the art of medicine and the skilful judge if he gives an erroneous judgement),[121] but not excused to one who is not qualified in that subject; or error which is not excused to any person whatever, and which is unbelief[122] if it concerns the principles of religion, or heresy[123] if it concerns something subordinate to the principles.

This [latter] error is that which occurs about [1] matters, knowledge of which is provided by all the different methods of indication,[124] so that knowledge of the matter in question is in this way possible for everyone. Examples are acknowledgement of God, Blessed and Exalted, of the prophetic missions, and of happiness and misery in the next life; for these three principles are attainable by
15 the three classes of indication, by which everyone without exception can come to assent to what he is obliged to know: I mean the rhetorical, dialectical and demonstrative indications. So whoever denies such a thing, when it is one of the principles of the Law, is an unbeliever, who persists in defiance with his tongue though

not with his heart, or neglects to expose himself to learning the indication of its truth. For if he belongs to the demonstrative class of men, a way has been provided for him to assent to it, by demonstration; if he belongs to the dialectical class, the way is by dialectic; and if he belongs to the class [which is convinced] by preaching, the way for him is by preaching. With this in view the Prophet, peace on him, said, 'I have been ordered to fight people until they say "There is no god but God" and believe in me'; he means, by any of the three methods of attaining belief that suits them.

[2] With regard to things which by reason of their recondite character are only knowable by demonstration, God has been gracious to those of His servants who have no access to demonstration, on account of their natures, habits or lack of facilities for education: He has coined for them images and likenesses[125] of these things, and summoned them to assent to those images, since it is possible for assent to those images to come about through the indications common to all men,[126] i.e. the dialectical and rhetorical indications. This is the reason why Scripture is divided into apparent and inner meanings: the apparent meaning consists of those images which are coined to stand for those ideas, while the inner meaning is those ideas [themselves], which are clear only to the demonstrative class. These are the four or five classes of beings mentioned by Abū Ḥāmid in *The book of the distinction*.[127]

[1] But when it happens, as we said, that we know the thing itself by the three methods, we do not need to coin images of it, and it remains true in its apparent meaning, not admitting allegorical interpretation.[128] If an apparent text of this kind refers to principles, anyone who interprets it allegorically is an unbeliever, e.g. anyone who thinks that there is no happiness or misery in the next life, and that the only purpose of this teaching is that men should be safeguarded from each other in their bodily and sensible lives, that it is but a practical device, and that man has no other goal than his sensible existence.[129]

If this is established, it will have become clear to you from what **16**
we have said that there are [1] apparent texts of Scripture which it is not permitted to interpret allegorically; to do so on fundamentals is unbelief, on subordinate matters, heresy.[130] There are also [2] apparent texts which have to be interpreted allegorically by men of the demonstrative class; for such men to take them in their apparent meaning is unbelief, while for those who are not of the demonstrative class to interpret them allegorically and take them out of their apparent meaning is unbelief or heresy on their part.[131]

Of this [latter] class are the verse about God's directing Himself and the Tradition about His descent.[132] That is why the Prophet, peace on him, said in the case of the black woman, when she told him that God was in the sky, 'Free her, for she is a believer'.[133] This was because she was not of the demonstrative class; and the reason for his decision was that the class of people to whom assent comes only through the imagination, i.e. who do not assent to a thing except in so far as they can imagine it, find it difficult to assent to the existence of a being which is unrelated to any imaginable thing.[134] This applies as well to those who understand from the relation stated[135] merely [that God has] a place; these are people who have advanced[136] a little in their thought beyond the position of the first class, ⟨by rejecting⟩ belief in corporeality.[137] Thus the [proper] answer to them with regard to such passages is that they belong to the ambiguous texts, and that the stop is to be placed after the words of God the Exalted 'And no one knows the interpretation thereof except God'.[138] The demonstrative class, while agreeing unanimously that this class of text must be interpreted allegorically, may disagree about the interpretation, according to the level of each one's knowledge of demonstration.

There is also [3] a third class of Scriptural texts falling uncertainly between the other two classes, on which there is doubt. One group of those who devote themselves to theoretical study attach them to the apparent texts which it is not permitted to interpret allegorically, others attach them to the texts with inner meanings which scholars are not permitted to take in their apparent meanings. This [divergence of opinions] is due to the difficulty and ambiguity of this class of text. Anyone who commits an error about this class is excused, I mean any scholar.

> [The texts about the future life fall into [3], since demonstrative scholars do not agree whether to take them in their apparent meaning or interpret them allegorically. Either is permissible. But it is inexcusable to deny the fact of a future life altogether.][139]

If it is asked, 'Since it is clear that scriptural texts in this respect fall into three grades, to which of these three grades, according to you, do the descriptions of the future life and its states belong?', we reply: The position clearly is that this matter belongs to the class
17 [3] about which there is disagreement. For we find a group of those who claim an affinity with demonstration saying that it is obligatory to take these passages in their apparent meaning, because there is no demonstration leading to the impossibility of the apparent meaning in them—this is the view of the Ash'arites; while another group of those who devote themselves to demonstration interpret these passages allegorically, and these people give the most diverse

interpretations of them. In this class must be counted Abū Ḥāmid and many of the Ṣūfīs; some of them combine the two interpretations of the passages,[140] as Abū Ḥāmid does in some of his books.

So it is likely that a scholar who commits an error in this matter is excused, while one who is correct receives thanks or a reward: that is, if he acknowledges the existence [of a future life] and merely gives a certain sort of allegorical interpretation, i.e. of the mode of the future life not of its existence, provided that the interpretation given does not lead to denial of its existence. In this matter only the negation of existence is unbelief, because it concerns one of the principles of religion and one of those points to which assent is attainable through the three methods common to 'the white man and the black man'.[141]

> [The unlearned classes must take such texts in their apparent meaning. It is unbelief for the learned to set down allegorical interpretations in popular writings. By doing this Ghazālī caused confusion among the people. Demonstrative books should be banned to the unqualified, but not to the learned.][142]

But anyone who is not a man of learning is obliged to take these passages in their apparent meaning, and allegorical interpretation of them is for him unbelief because it *leads to* unbelief. That is why we hold that, for anyone whose duty it is to believe in the apparent meaning, allegorical interpretation is unbelief, because it leads to unbelief. Anyone of the interpretative class who discloses such [an interpretation] to him is summoning him to unbelief, and he who summons to unbelief is an unbeliever.

Therefore allegorical interpretations ought to be set down only in demonstrative books, because if they are in demonstrative books they are encountered by no one but men of the demonstrative class. But if they are set down in other than demonstrative books and one deals with them by poetical, rhetorical or dialectical methods, as Abū Ḥāmid does,[143] then he commits an offence against the Law and against philosophy, even though the fellow intended nothing but good. For by this procedure he wanted to increase the number of learned men, but in fact he increased the number of the corrupted not of the learned! As a result, one group came to slander philosophy, another to slander religion, and another to reconcile the [first] two [groups].[144] It seems that this [last] was one of his objects in his books; an indication that he wanted **18**
by this [procedure] to arouse minds is that he adhered to no one doctrine in his books but was an Ash'arite with the Ash'arites, a Ṣūfī with the Ṣūfīs and a philosopher with the philosophers, so that he was like the man in the verse:

'One day a Yamanī, if I meet a man of Yaman,
And if I meet a Ma'addī, I'm an 'Adnānī.'[145]

The *imāms* of the Muslims ought to forbid those of his books which contain learned matter to all save the learned, just as they ought to forbid demonstrative books to those who are not capable of understanding them. But the damage done to people by demonstrative books is lighter, because for the most part only persons of superior natural intelligence become acquainted with demonstrative books, and this class of persons is only misled through lack of practical virtue, unorganized reading, and tackling them without a teacher.[146] On the other hand their total prohibition obstructs the purpose to which the Law summons, because it is a wrong to the best class of people and the best class of beings. For to do justice to the best class of beings demands that they should be known profoundly, by persons equipped to know them profoundly, and these are the best class of people; and the greater the value of the being, the greater is the injury towards it, which consists of ignorance of it. Thus the Exalted has said, 'Associating [other gods] with God is indeed a great wrong.'[147]

[We have only discussed these questions in a popular work because they were already being publicly discussed.]

This is as much as we see fit to affirm in this field of study, i.e. the correspondence between religion and philosophy and the rules for allegorical interpretation in religion. If it were not for the publicity given to the matter and to these questions which we have discussed, we should not have permitted ourselves to write a word on the subject;[148] and we should not have had to make excuses for doing so to the interpretative scholars, because the proper place to discuss these questions is in demonstrative books. God is the Guide and helps us to follow the right course!

[Chapter Three]

[PHILOSOPHICAL INTERPRETATIONS OF SCRIPTURE SHOULD NOT BE TAUGHT TO THE MAJORITY. THE LAW PROVIDES OTHER METHODS OF INSTRUCTING THEM.]

[The purpose of Scripture is to teach true theoretical and practical science and right practice and attitudes.]

You ought to know that the purpose of Scripture is simply to teach true science and right practice. True science is knowledge of God, Blessed and Exalted, and the other beings as they really are, and especially of noble beings,[149] and knowledge of happiness and misery in the next life.[150] Right practice consists in performing **19**
the acts which bring happiness and avoiding the acts which bring misery;[151] and it is knowledge of these acts that is called 'practical science'. They fall into two divisions: (1) outward bodily acts; the science of these is called 'jurisprudence'; and (2) acts of the soul such as gratitude, patience and other moral attitudes which the Law enjoins or forbids; the science of these is called 'asceticism' or 'the sciences of the future life'. To these Abū Ḥāmid turned his attention in his book: as people had given up this sort [of act] and become immersed in the other sort,[152] and as this sort [2] involves the greater fear of God, which is the cause of happiness, he called his book '*The revival of the sciences of religion*'.[153] But we have digressed from our subject, so let us return to it.

[Scripture teaches concepts both directly and by symbols, and uses demonstrative, dialectical and rhetorical arguments. Dialectical and rhetorical arguments are prevalent because the main aim of Scripture is to teach the majority. In these arguments concepts are indicated directly or by symbols, in various combinations in premisses and conclusion.]

We say: The purpose of Scripture is to teach true science and right practice; and teaching is of two classes, [of] concepts and [of] judgements,[154] as the logicians[155] have shown. Now the methods available to men of [arriving at] judgements are three: demonstrative, dialectical and rhetorical;[156] and the methods of forming concepts are two: either [conceiving] the object itself or [conceiving] a symbol of it.[157] But not everyone has the natural ability to take in demonstrations, or [even] dialectical arguments, let alone demonstrative arguments which are so hard to learn and need so much time [even] for those who are qualified to learn them. Therefore, since it is the purpose of Scripture simply to teach everyone, Scripture has to contain every method of [bringing about] judgements of assent and every method of forming concepts.

Now some of the methods of assent comprehend the majority of people, i.e. the occurrence of assent as a result of them [is comprehensive]: these are the rhetorical and the dialectical [methods] —and the rhetorical is more comprehensive than the dialectical. Another method is peculiar to a smaller number of people: this is the demonstrative. Therefore, since the primary purpose of Scripture is to take care of the majority (without neglecting to arouse the élite), the prevailing methods of expression in religion are the common methods by which the majority comes to form concepts and judgements.[158]

These [common] methods in religion are of four classes:[159]

One of them occurs where the method is common, yet specialized[160] in two respects: i.e. where it is certain in its concepts and judgements, in spite of being rhetorical or dialectical. These syllogisms are those whose premisses, in spite of being based on accepted ideas or on opinions,[161] are accidentally certain, and whose conclusions are accidentally to be taken in their direct meaning without symbolization. Scriptural texts of this class have no allegorical interpretations, and anyone who denies them or interprets them allegorically is an unbeliever.

The second class occurs where the premisses, in spite of being based on accepted ideas or on opinions, are certain, and where the conclusions are symbols for the things which it was intended to conclude. [Texts of] this [class], i.e. their conclusions, admit of allegorical interpretation.

The third is the reverse of this: it occurs where the conclusions are the very things which it was intended to conclude, while the premisses are based on accepted ideas or on opinions without being accidentally certain. [Texts of] this [class] also, i.e. their conclusions, do not admit of allegorical interpretation, but their premisses may do so.

The fourth [class] occurs where the premisses are based on accepted ideas or opinions, without being accidentally certain, and where the conclusions are symbols for what it was intended to conclude. In these cases the duty of the élite is to interpret them allegorically, while the duty of the masses is to take them in their apparent meaning.

[Where symbols are used, each class of men, demonstrative, dialectical and rhetorical, must try to understand the inner meaning symbolized or rest content with the apparent meaning, according to their capacities.]

In general, everything in these [texts] which admits of allegorical interpretation can only be understood by demonstration. The duty of the élite here is to apply such interpretation; while the duty of the masses is to take them in their apparent meaning in both respects, i.e. in concept and judgement, since their natural capacity does not allow more than that.

But there may occur to students of Scripture allegorical interpretations due to the superiority of one of the common methods over another in [bringing about] assent, i.e. when the indication contained in the allegorical interpretation is more persuasive than the indication contained in the apparent meaning. Such interpretations are popular;[162] and [the making of them] is possibly a duty for those whose powers of theoretical understanding have
attained the dialectical level. To this sort belong some of the **21**
interpretations of the Ash'arites and Mu'tazilites—though the Mu'tazilites are generally sounder in their statements.[163] The masses on the other hand, who are incapable of more than rhetorical arguments, have the duty of taking these [texts] in their apparent meaning, and they are not permitted to know such interpretations at all.

Thus people in relation to Scripture fall into three classes:

One class is those who are not people of interpretation at all: these are the rhetorical class. They are the overwhelming mass, for no man of sound intellect is exempted from this kind of assent.[164]

Another class is the people of dialectical interpretation: these are the dialecticians, either by nature alone or by nature and habit.

Another class is the people of certain interpretation: these are the demonstrative class, by nature and training,[165] i.e. in the art of philosophy. This interpretation ought not to be expressed to the dialectical class, let alone to the masses.

[To explain the inner meaning to people unable to understand it is to destroy their belief in the apparent meaning without putting anything in its place. The result is unbelief in learners and teachers. It is best for the learned to profess ignorance, quoting the *Qur'ān* on the limitations of man's understanding.]

When something of these allegorical interpretations is expressed to anyone unfit to receive them—especially demonstrative interpretations because of their remoteness from common knowledge—both he who expresses it and he to whom it is expressed are led into unbelief. The reason for that [in the case of the latter][166] is that allegorical interpretation comprises two things, rejection of the apparent meaning and affirmation of the allegorical one; so that if the apparent meaning is rejected in the mind of someone who can only grasp apparent meanings, without the allegorical meaning being affirmed in his mind, the result is unbelief, if it [the text in question] concerns the principles of religion.

Allegorical interpretations, then, ought not to be expressed to the masses nor set down in rhetorical or dialectical books, i.e. books containing arguments of these two sorts, as was done by Abū Ḥāmid. They should ⟨not⟩ be expressed to this class; and with regard to an apparent text, when there is a ⟨self-evident⟩ doubt whether it is apparent to everyone and whether knowledge of its interpretation is impossible for them, they should be told that it is ambiguous[167] and [its meaning] known by no one except God; and that the stop should be put here in the sentence of the Exalted, 'And no one knows the interpretation thereof except God'.[168] The same kind of answer should also be given to a question about abstruse matters, which there is no way for the masses to understand; just as the Exalted has answered in His saying, 'And they will ask you about the Spirit. Say, "The Spirit is by the command of my Lord; you have been given only a little knowledge" '.[169]

[Certain people have injured the masses particularly, by giving them allegorical interpretations which are false. These people are exactly analogous to bad medical advisers. The true doctor is related to bodily health in the same way as the Legislator to spiritual health, which the *Qur'ān* teaches us to pursue. The true allegory is "the deposit" mentioned in the *Qur'ān*.]

22 As for the man who expresses these allegories to unqualified persons, he is an unbeliever on account of his summoning people to unbelief.[170] This is contrary to the summons of the Legislator,[171] especially when they are false allegories concerning the principles of religion, as has happened in the case of a group of people of our time.[172] For we have seen some of them thinking that they were being philosophic and that they perceived, with their remarkable wisdom, things which conflict with Scripture in every respect, i.e. [in passages] which do not admit of allegorical interpretation; and that it was obligatory to express these things to the masses.

But by expressing those false beliefs to the masses they have been a cause of perdition to the masses and themselves, in this world and the next.[173]

The relation between the aim of these people and the aim of the Legislator [can be illustrated by] a parable,[174] of a man who goes to a skilful doctor. [This doctor's] aim is to preserve the health and cure the diseases of all the people, by prescribing for them rules which can be commonly accepted, about the necessity of using the things which will preserve their health and cure their diseases, and avoiding the opposite things. He is unable to make them all doctors, because a doctor is one who knows by demonstrative methods the things which preserve health and cure disease. Now this [man whom we have mentioned] goes out to the people and tells them, 'These methods prescribed by this doctor for you are not right'; and he sets out to discredit them, so that they are rejected by the people. Or he says, 'They have allegorical interpretations'; but the people neither understand these nor assent to them in practice. Well, do you think that people in this condition will do any of the things which are useful for preserving health and curing disease, or that this man who has persuaded them to reject what they formerly believed in will now be able to use those [things] with them, I mean for preserving health? No, he will be unable to use those [things] with them, nor will they use them, and so they will all perish.

This [is what will happen] if he expresses to them true allegories[175] about those matters, because of their inability to understand them; let alone if he expresses to them false allegories, because this will lead them to think that there are no such things as health which ought to be preserved and disease which ought to be cured—let alone that there are things which preserve health and cure disease.[176] **23**
It is the same when someone expresses allegories to the masses, and to those who are not qualified to understand them, in the sphere of Scripture; thus he makes it appear false and turns people away from it; and he who turns people away from Scripture is an unbeliever.

Indeed this comparison is certain,[177] not poetic as one might suppose. It presents a true analogy, in that the relation of the doctor to the health of bodies is [the same as] the relation of the Legislator to the health of souls: i.e. the doctor is he who seeks to preserve the health of bodies when it exists and to restore it when it is lost, while the Legislator is he who desires this [end] for the health of souls.[178] This health is what is called 'fear of God'. The precious Book has told us to seek it by acts conformable to the Law, in several verses. Thus the Exalted has said, 'Fasting has been prescribed for you, as it was prescribed for those who were before you;

perhaps you will fear God.'[179] Again the Exalted has said, 'Their flesh and their blood shall not touch God, but your fear shall touch him';[180] 'Prayer prevents immorality and transgression';[181] and other verses to the same effect contained in the precious Book. Through knowledge of Scripture and practice according to Scripture the Legislator aims solely at this health; and it is from this health that happiness in the future life follows, just as misery in the future life follows from its opposite.

From this it will be clear to you that true allegories ought not to be set down in popular books, let alone false ones. The true allegory is the deposit which man was charged to hold and which he held, and from which all beings shied away, i.e. that which is mentioned in the words of the Exalted, 'We offered the deposit to the heavens, the earth and the mountains', [and so on to the end of] the verse.[182]

> [It was due to the wrong use of allegorical interpretation by the Mu'tazilites and Ash'arites that hostile sects arose in Islam.]

It was due to allegorical interpretations—especially the false ones—and the supposition that such interpretations of Scripture ought to be expressed to everyone, that the sects of Islam arose, with the result that each one accused the others of unbelief or heresy. Thus the Mu'tazilites interpreted many verses and Traditions allegorically, and expressed their interpretations to the masses,
24 and the Ash'arites did the same, although they used such interpretations less frequently.[183] In consequence they threw people into hatred, mutual detestation and wars, tore the Scriptures to shreds, and completely divided people.[184]

In addition to all this, in the methods which they followed to establish their interpretations they neither went along with the masses nor with the élite: not with the masses, because their methods were ⟨more⟩ obscure than the methods common to the majority, and not with the élite, because if these methods are inspected they are found deficient in the conditions [required] for demonstration,[185] as will be understood after the slightest inspection by anyone acquainted with the conditions of demonstration. Further, many of the principles on which the Ash'arites based their knowledge are sophistical,[186] for they deny many necessary truths such as the permanence of accidents, the action of things on other things, the existence of necessary causes for effects, of substantial forms, and of secondary causes.[187]

And their theorists wronged the Muslims in this sense, that a sect of Ash'arites called an unbeliever anyone who did not attain knowledge of the existence of the Glorious Creator by the methods laid down by them in their books for attaining this knowledge. But in truth it is they who are the unbelievers and in error! From this point they proceeded to disagree, one group saying 'The primary obligation is theoretical study', another group saying 'It is belief'; i.e. [this happened] because they did not know which are the methods common to everyone, through whose doors the Law has summoned all people [to enter]; they supposed that there was only one method. Thus they mistook the aim of the Legislator, and were both themselves in error and led others into error.

[The proper methods for teaching the people are indicated in the *Qur'ān*, as the early Muslims knew. The popular portions of the Book are miraculous in providing for the needs of every class of mind. We intend to make a study of its teachings at the apparent level, and thus help to remedy the grievous harm done by ignorant partisans of philosophy and religion.]

It may be asked: 'If these methods followed by the Ash'arites and other theorists are not the common methods by which the Legislator has aimed to teach the masses, and by which alone it is possible to teach them, then what are those [common] methods in this religion of ours'? We reply: They are exclusively the methods set down in the precious Book. For if the precious Book is inspected, there will be found in it the three methods that are available for all the people, ⟨namely⟩ the common methods for the instruction of the majority of the people and the special method.[188] And if their merits are inspected, it becomes apparent that no better common methods for the instruction of the masses can be found than the methods mentioned in it.

Thus whoever tampers with them, by making an allegorical interpretation not apparent in itself, or [at least] not more apparent to everyone than they are (and that [greater apparency] is something non-existent), is rejecting their wisdom and rejecting their **25**
intended effects in procuring human happiness. This is very apparent from [a comparison of] the condition of the first believers with the condition of those who came after them. For the first believers arrived at perfect virtue and fear of God only by using these sayings [of Scripture] without interpreting them allegorically; and anyone of them who did find out an allegorical interpretation did not think fit to express it [to others]. But when those who came after them used allegorical interpretation, their fear of God grew less, their dissensions increased, their love for one another was removed, and they became divided into sects.

So whoever wishes to remove this heresy from religion should direct his attention to the precious Book, and glean from it the indications present [in it] concerning everything in turn that it obliges us to believe, and exercise his judgement in looking at its apparent meaning as well as he is able, without interpreting any of it allegorically, except where the allegorical meaning is apparent in itself, i.e. commonly apparent to everyone.[189] For if the sayings set down in Scripture for the instruction of the people are inspected, it seems that in mastering their meaning[190] one arrives at a point, beyond which none but a man of the demonstrative class can extract from their apparent wording a meaning which is not apparent in them.[191] This property is not found in any other sayings.

For those religious sayings in the precious Book which are expressed to everyone have three properties that indicate their miraculous character:[192] (1) There exist none more completely persuasive and convincing to everyone than they. (2) Their meaning admits naturally of mastery, up to a point beyond which their allegorical interpretation (when they are of a kind to have such an interpretation) can only be found out by the demonstrative class. (3) They contain means of drawing the attention of the people of truth to the true allegorical meaning.[193] This [character] is not found in the doctrines of the Ash'arites nor in those of the Mu'tazilites, i.e. their interpretations do not admit of mastery nor contain [means of] drawing attention to the truth, nor are they true; and this is why heresies have multiplied.

It is our desire to devote our time to this object and achieve it effectively,[194] and if God grants us a respite of life we shall work steadily towards it in so far as this is made possible for us; and it may be that that work will serve as a starting point for our successors. For our soul is in the utmost sorrow and pain by reason
26 of the evil fancies and perverted beliefs which have infiltrated this religion, and particularly such [afflictions] as have happened to it at the hands of people who claim an affinity with philosophy.[195] For injuries from a friend are more severe than injuries from an enemy. I refer to the fact that philosophy is the friend and milk-sister of religion; thus injuries from people related to philosophy are the severest injuries [to religion]—apart from the enmity, hatred and quarrels which such [injuries] stir up between the two, which are companions by nature and lovers by essence and instinct. It has also been injured by a host of ignorant friends who claim an affinity with it: these are the sects which exist within it. But God directs all men aright and helps everyone to love Him; He unites their hearts in the fear of Him, and removes from them hatred and loathing by His grace and His mercy!

Indeed God has already removed many of these ills, ignorant ideas and misleading practices, by means of this triumphant rule.[196]

By it He has opened a way to many benefits, especially to the class of persons who have trodden the path of study and sought to know the truth. This [He has done] by summoning the masses to a middle way of knowing God the Glorious, [a way] which is raised above the low level of the followers of authority[197] but is below the turbulence of the theologians; and by drawing the attention of the élite to their obligation to make a thorough study of the principles of religion. God is the Giver of success and the Guide by His Goodness.

[Appendix: *Ḍamīma*][198]

128

THE QUESTION MENTIONED BY THE *SHAYKH* ABUL-WALĪD IN *THE DECISIVE TREATISE*

[We shall try to solve your problem about God's Knowledge.]

May God prolong your power, continue to bless you, and keep you out of sight of misfortunes![199]

By your superior intelligence and abundant talents you have surpassed many of those who devote their lives to these sciences, and your sure insight has led you to become aware of the difficulty that arises about the eternal, Glorious Knowledge,[200] on account of Its being connected with the things originated by It. It is therefore our obligation, in the interests of truth and of ending your perplexity, to resolve this difficulty, after formulating it; for he who does not know how to tie a knot cannot untie it.[201]

[The problem: How can God be aware of a change in reality without a corresponding change occurring in His eternal Knowledge?]

The difficulty is compelling, as follows. If all these things were in the Knowledge of God the Glorious before they existed, are they in their state of existence [the same] in His Knowledge as they were before their existence, or are they in their state of existence other in His Knowledge than they were before they existed? If we say that in their state of existence they are other in God's Knowledge than they were before they existed, it follows that the eternal Knowledge is subject to change, and that when they pass from non-existence to existence, there comes into existence additional Knowledge: but that is impossible for the eternal Knowledge.[202] If on the other hand we say that the Knowledge of them in both states is one and the same, it will be asked, 'Are they in themselves', i.e. the beings which come into existence, 'the same before they exist as when they exist?' The answer will have to be 'No, in themselves they are not the same before they exist as when they exist'; otherwise the existent and the non-existent[203] would be one and the

same. If the adversary admits this, he can be asked, 'Is not true knowledge acquaintance with existence as it really is?' If he says 'Yes', it will be said, 'Consequently if the object varies in itself, 129
the knowledge of it must vary; otherwise it will not be known as it really is'. Thus one of two alternatives is necessary: either the eternal Knowledge varies in Itself, or the things that come into existence are not known to It. But both alternatives are impossible for God the Glorious.

This difficulty is confirmed by what appears in the case of man: His knowledge of non-existent things depends on the supposition of existence, while his knowledge of them when they exist depends ⟨on existence itself⟩. For it is self-evident that the two states of knowledge are different; otherwise he would be ignorant of things' existence at the time when they exist.

[God's foreknowledge of all change does not solve the problem, as the theologians think, for the actual occurrence of the change presumably adds something new to His Knowledge.]

It is impossible to escape from this [difficulty] by the usual answer of the theologians about it, that God the Exalted knows things before their existence as they will be at the time of their existence, in respect of time, place and other attributes proper to each being. For it can be said to them: 'Then when they come to exist, does there occur any change or not?'—with reference to the passage of the thing from non-existence to existence. If they say 'No change occurs', they are merely being supercilious. But if they say 'There does occur a change', it can be said to them: 'Then is the occurrence of this change known to the eternal Knowledge or not?' Thus the difficulty is compelling. In sum, it can hardly be conceived that the knowledge of a thing before it exists can be identical with the knowledge of it after it exists. Such, then, is the formulation of this problem in its strongest possible form, as we have explained it to you in conversation.[204]

[Nor is Ghazālī's solution satisfactory. He regards God's Knowledge as a term in a relation, which does not change in itself when that to which it is related, the known object, changes its relation to it. But knowledge is a relation, not a related term.]

The [full] solution of this difficulty would call for a lengthy discourse; but here we shall only go into the decisive point of the solution. Abū Ḥāmid in his book entitled *The disintegration* wanted

to resolve this difficulty in a way which carries no conviction.[205] He stated an argument the gist of which is as follows. He asserted that knowledge and the object known are related; and as one of two related things may change without the other changing in itself, this is just what seems to happen to things in the Knowledge of God the Glorious: they change in themselves, but the Knowledge of God the Glorious about them does not change. A parallel case
130 of related things would be if a single column were first on the right of Zayd and then came to be on his left: meanwhile Zayd[206] would not have changed in himself. But this [argument] is not correct. For the relation has changed in itself: the relation which was a right-handed one has become a left-handed one, and the only thing which has not changed is the subject of the relation, i.e. its bearer, Zayd. If this is so, and knowledge is the relation itself, it must necessarily change when the object known changes, just as, when the column changes [its position], the relation of the column to Zayd changes, coming to be a left-handed relation after having been a right-handed one.

> [The correct solution is that the eternal Knowledge is the cause of beings, not their effect as originated knowledge is. Therefore It does not change when they change.]

The way to resolve this difficulty, in our opinion, is to recognize that the position of the eternal Knowledge with respect to beings is different from the position of originated knowledge with respect to beings, in that the existence of beings is a cause and reason for our knowledge, while the eternal Knowledge is a cause and reason for beings. If, when beings come to exist after not having existed, there occurred an addition in the eternal Knowledge such as occurs in originated knowledge, it would follow that the eternal Knowledge would be an effect of beings, not their cause. Therefore there must not occur any change such as occurs in originated knowledge. The mistake in this matter has arisen simply from making an analogy between the eternal Knowledge and originated knowledge, i.e. between the suprasensible and the sensible; and the falsity of this analogy is well known. Just as no change occurs in an agent when his act comes into being, i.e. no change which has not already occurred, so no change occurs in the eternal Glorious Knowledge when the object of Its Knowledge results from It.

Thus the difficulty is resolved, and we do not have to admit that if there occurs no change, i.e. in the eternal Knowledge, He does not know beings at the time of their coming into existence just as they are; we only have to admit that He does not know them with originated knowledge but with eternal Knowledge.

For the occurrence of change in knowledge when beings change is a condition only of knowledge which is caused by beings, i.e. originated knowledge.

[The philosophers hold that God knows particulars with eternal Knowledge, not that He does not know them at all. Indeed, they consider that His knowledge is the cause of their coming into existence, also that It sends premonitions of particulars in dreams.]

Therefore eternal Knowledge is only connected with beings in 131
a manner other than that in which originated knowledge is connected with them. This does not mean that It is not connected at all, as the philosophers have been accused of saying, in the context of this difficulty, that the Glorious One does not know particulars. Their position is not what has been imputed to them; rather they hold that He does not know particulars with originated knowledge, the occurrence of which is conditioned by their occurrence, since He is a cause of them, not caused by them as originated knowledge is. This is the furthest extent to which purification [of concepts][207] ought to be admitted.

For demonstration compels the conclusion that He knows things, because their issuing from Him is solely due to His knowing; it is not due to His being merely Existent or Existent with a certain attribute, but to His knowing, as the Exalted has said: 'Does He not know, He who created? He is the Penetrating, the Omniscient!'[208] But demonstration also compels the conclusion that He does not know things with a knowledge of the same character as originated knowledge. Therefore there must be another knowledge of beings which is unqualified,[209] the eternal Glorious Knowledge. And how is it conceivable that the Peripatetic philosophers could have held that the eternal Knowledge does not comprehend particulars, when they held that It is the cause of warning in dreams, of revelation, and of other kinds of inspiration?[210]

[Conclusion]

This is the way to resolve this difficulty, as it appears to us; and what has been said is incontestable and indubitable. It is God who helps us to follow the right course and directs us to the truth. Peace on you, with the mercy and blessings of God.

[Extract: *Kitāb al-kashf 'an manāhij al-adilla*, pp. 122-27]

[THE FUTURE LIFE][211]

[Corporeal symbols are more effective than spiritual ones in instructing the masses about the life beyond, and are used in the *Qur'ān* which is primarily concerned with the majority.][212]

122 All religions, as we have said, agree on the fact that souls experience states of happiness or misery after death,[213] but they disagree in the manner of symbolizing these states and explaining their existence to men. And it seems that the [kind of] symbolization which is found in this religion of ours is the most perfect means of explanation to the majority of men, and provides the greatest stimulus to their souls to [pursue the goals of] the life beyond; and the primary concern of religions is with the majority. Spiritual symbolization, on the other hand, seems to provide less stimulus to the souls of the masses towards [the goals of] the life beyond, and the masses have less desire and fear of it than they do of corporeal symbolization. Therefore it seems that corporeal symbolization provides a stronger stimulus to [the goals of] the life beyond than spiritual; the spiritual [kind] is more acceptable to the class of debating theologians, but they are the minority.

[There are three interpretations of the symbols by Muslims. (1) The life beyond is the same in kind as this one, but it is permanent, not limited in duration. (2) It differs in kind: (a) The life beyond is spiritual, and is only symbolized by sensible images for the purpose of exposition. (b) It is corporeal, but the bodies are other, immortal ones not these perishable ones. This opinion is suitable for the élite. It avoids the absurdity of (1), arising from the fact that our bodies here provide material for other earthly bodies and so cannot at the same time exist in the other world. But every opinion is permissible except total rejection of another life.]

For this reason we find the people of Islam divided into three sects with regard to the understanding of the symbolization which is used in [the texts of] our religion referring to the states of the future life. One sect holds that that existence is identical with this

existence here with respect to bliss and pleasure, i.e. they hold that it is of the same sort and that the two existences differ only in respect of permanence and limit of duration, i.e. the former is permanent and the latter of limited duration. Another group holds that there is a difference in the kind of existence. This [group] is divided into two subdivisions. One [sub-] group holds that the existence symbolized by these sensible images is spiritual, and that it has been symbolized thus only for the purpose of exposition; these people are supported by many well-known arguments from Scripture, but there would be no point in enumerating them.[214] Another [sub-] group thinks that it is corporeal, but believes that that corporeality existing in the life beyond differs from the corporeality of this life in that the latter is perishable while the former 123
is immortal. They too are supported by arguments from Scripture, and it seems that Ibn ʿAbbās was one of those who held this opinion, for he is reported to have said, 'There is nothing in this lower world like the next world except the names.'[215]

It seems that this opinion is more suitable for the élite;[216] for the admissibility of this opinion is founded on facts which are not discussed in front of everyone. One is that the soul is immortal. The second is that the return of the soul to other bodies[217] does not involve the same absurdity as ⟨its⟩ return ⟨to⟩ those same [earthly] bodies. This is because it is apparent that the materials of the bodies that exist here are successively transferred from one body to another: i.e. one and the same material exists in many persons at different times. Bodies like these cannot possibly all exist actually [at the same time], because their material is one: for instance, a man dies, his body is transformed into dust, that dust is transformed into a plant, another man feeds on that plant; then semen proceeds from him, from which another man is born. But if other bodies are supposed, this state of affairs[218] does not follow as a consequence.

The truth in this question is that every man's duty is [to believe] whatever his study of it leads him to [conclude], provided that it is not such a study as would cause him to reject the principle altogether, by denying the existence [of the future life] altogether; for this manner of belief obliges us to call its holder an unbeliever, because the existence of this [future] state for man is made known to people through their Scriptures and their intellects.[219]

[The basic assumption of all the permissible views is the immortality of the soul. It can be proved from the *Qur'ān*, which equates death with sleep; now since we know that the soul is not dissolved in sleep, the same applies to death. In both cases the organ, not the soul itself, ceases.][220]

The whole of this [argument] is founded on the immortality of the soul. If it is asked 'Does Scripture contain an indication of the immortality of the soul or [at least] a hint of it?', we reply: This is found in the precious Book in the words of the Exalted, 'God receives the souls at the time of their death, and those which have not died He receives in their sleep', [and so on to the end of] the verse.[221] The significant aspect of this verse is that in it He has equated sleep and death with respect to the annihilation of the soul's activity. Thus if the cessation of the soul's activity in death were due to the soul's dissolution, not to a change in the soul's
124 organ, the cessation of its activity in sleep [too] would have to be due to the dissolution of its essential being; but if that were the case, it would not return on waking to its normal condition. So since it does return to it, we know that this cessation does not happen to it through anything which attaches to it in its substantial nature, but is only something which attaches to it owing to a cessation of its organ; and [we know] that it does not follow that if the organ ceases the soul must cease. Death *is* a cessation; it must therefore be of the organ, as is the case in sleep. As the Philosopher says, 'If the old man were to find an eye like the young man's eye, he would see as the young man sees'.[222]

This is as much as we see fit to affirm in our investigation of the beliefs of this religion of ours, the religion of Islam.

[ALLEGORICAL INTERPRETATION]

[Texts of Scripture fall into the following classes:

(1) Where the apparent meaning is the meaning really intended. Such texts may not be interpreted allegorically.

(2) Where there is symbolization:

- (i) Where it is difficult to know both that there is symbolization and what is symbolized. Such texts may be interpreted allegorically only by the learned.
- (ii) Where it is easy to know both that there is symbolization and what is symbolized. Such texts must be interpreted allegorically by everyone.
- (iii) Where it is easy to know that there is symbolization but difficult to know what is symbolized. In these cases the masses must be told that only the learned are able to understand the true interpretation; or they must be given an easy allegorical explanation, according to the rules laid down by Ghazālī.

(iv) Where it is difficult to know that there is symbolization, but easy to know what it symbolizes. In these cases it is preferable to deny the existence of symbolization. When it is made known, the resulting popular beliefs are apt to cause confusion.][223]

It now remains for us out of our programme only to study what portions of Scripture it is permissible and what it is not permissible to interpret allegorically, and, when it is permissible, to whom the permission is given. With this [topic] we shall conclude the argument of this book.

We say that the ideas found in Scripture fall into five classes: i.e. they are divided into two primary classes, and the second of the two is divisible into four [sub-] classes.

[1] The first, indivisible class consists of [the cases] where the idea which is [outwardly] expressed is identical with the idea really intended.[224]

[2] The second, divisible class consists of [the cases] where the idea expressed in Scripture is not the idea really intended, but is merely substituted for it as a means of symbolization.[225] This class is divided into four parts. [i] The first is where the idea, which is expressed by its symbol, is known ⟨in⟩ its reality only by difficult composite syllogisms, taking a long time and many skills to learn, and which superior minds alone can grasp; and where the fact that the symbol expressed is distinct from the thing symbolized is known only with as much difficulty as that we have [just] described. [ii] The second is the opposite of this, where it is easy to know both things, i.e. that what is expressed is a symbol, and what it symbolizes. [iii] The third is where it is easy to know that it is a symbol for something, but difficult to know what it symbolizes. [iv] The fourth is the reverse of this, where it is easy to know what it symbolizes **125**
but difficult to know [in the first place] that it is a symbol.[226]

Now it is undoubtedly an error to interpret allegorically [1] the first of the two primary classes.

In the case of [2, i] the first [sub-]class of the second[class], that which is difficult in both respects, allegorical interpretation is the special task of 'those who are well grounded in science', and it is not permitted to be expressed to any but 'the well grounded'.

[ii] In the opposite class, that which is easy in both respects, an allegorical interpretation is intended and it is obligatory to express it.

[iii] ⟨In the third class the case is otherwise,⟩ because in this class on account of its difficulty symbolization does not occur for the purpose of explanation to the masses, but only occurs to stimulate souls towards to it.[227] Thus for example in the words of the

Prophet, peace on him, 'The Black Stone is the right hand of God on earth',[228] and other similar sayings, it is self-evident or easily known that there is a symbol, but it is difficult to know what it symbolizes. Therefore such [a text] ought not to be interpreted allegorically by any but the élite and the scholars; and those who notice that it is symbolic, without being of the class of people who can understand what it symbolizes, should either be told that it is of the ambiguous kind whose meaning is known by the well grounded scholars, or the symbolization in it should be translated for them into something [even] easier than what they know, the fact that it is symbolic. The latter course seems more suitable as a means of ending the doubt which arises in the soul from this [class of text].

The rule in this regard is that which was followed by Abū Ḥāmid in *The book of the distinction*:[229] that this class of persons should learn that one and the same thing has five [modes of] existence, which are called by Abū Ḥāmid 'essential', 'sensible', 'imaginary', 'intellectual' and 'metaphorical'. Thus when the question arises one considers which of these four [last-named modes of] existence is more persuasive[230] to the class of persons who find it impossible [to believe] that what is meant by it is essential existence, i.e. that which is external; then he brings down this symbolization for them to [the level of] that [mode of] existence whose possibility is most acceptable to their way of thinking. To this sort [of texts] belong the words of the Prophet, peace on him, 'There is nothing that I have not seen, but I have seen it already in this place of mine—even Paradise and the Fire';[231] and 'Between
126 my basin and my pulpit there is one of the gardens of Paradise, and my pulpit is close by my basin';[232] and 'Dust consumes all of a son of Adam except his *os coccygis*'.[233] It is easy to perceive that all these sayings are symbolic, but difficult to perceive what they symbolize. Thus to the class [of people] who notice this much, these sayings ought to be brought down to that one of those four modes of existence which most nearly resembles [the essential mode].

This manner of interpretation, if it is employed in these contexts and in this way, is authorized by Scripture; but if it is employed in other contexts, it is an error. Abū Ḥāmid did not make such a distinction: for instance [2, i] when it is difficult to understand the context in both respects, i.e. that it is a symbol and what it symbolizes, but there arises at first glance a suspicion of the imagination that it is symbolic. That suspicion is idle;[234] therefore in such a case that suspicion ought to be discredited and it [the text] should not be made an object of allegorical interpretation, as has happened in so many contexts (as I have shown you in this book) at the hands of the theologians, i.e. the Ashʿarites and Muʿtazilites.

[iv] The fourth class is the opposite of this: that in which it is difficult to know that it [the text] is symbolic, but when once it is admitted that it is symbolic, it easily becomes apparent what it symbolizes. Here again we must be circumspect in giving allegorical interpretations, i.e. among the class [of people] who, if they perceive that it is symbolic, perceive what it symbolizes, but who only perceive that it is symbolic through a suspicion or persuasion, since they are not scholars, 'well grounded in science'. So it is possible to say that the surest way to maintain respect for Scripture is not to interpret these [texts] allegorically, and to discredit in the minds of these people the things through which they have come to think that such sayings are symbolic; and this is the most suitable course.

It is also possible to release the allegorical interpretation to them, because of the strong resemblance between the thing mentioned and what it symbolizes. However, when allegorical interpretations of these two classes [of texts] [iii and iv] are declared openly, they give birth to strange beliefs, remote from the apparent meaning of Scripture; and sometimes these become widespread, until they are denied by the masses. This is what happened to the Ṣūfīs and to those scholars who followed this path: when allegorical interpretation of this Scripture was controlled by men who did not 127
distinguish either these contexts or the class of people to whom it is permissible to give allegorical interpretations, the situation became confused, and various sects arose among them, each accusing the other of unbelief; and all this is ignorance of the purpose of the Law and transgression against it.

[Conclusion]

From our account you have now become aware of the amount of error that occurs as a result of allegorical interpretation. It is our desire to have the chance to fulfil this aim with regard to all the statements of Scripture: i.e. to discuss which of them have to be interpreted allegorically and which not, and, when they have to be interpreted, to whom the interpretations should be given; I mean, [to deal thus] with every difficult passage in the *Qur'ān* and the Traditions, and show the place of all the statements in these four classes.[235] But the aim which we have pursued in this book is now accomplished; and we have given it precedence only because we have held it to be the most important of aims connected with Scripture. It is God who helps us to follow the right course and guarantees our reward, through His favour and mercy. This book was concluded in the year 575.[236]

NOTES TO THE TRANSLATION

References are to the pages and lines of Müller's Arabic edition, indicated in the margins of my translation as well as in my Arabic edition (Leiden, 1959).

[1] 1.1. "The decisive treatise": *Kitāb faṣl al-maqāl*, lit. "The book of the decision of the discourse."

"religion": *ash-sharīʿa*, usually somewhat broader than *ash-sharʿ*.

"philosophy": *al-ḥikma*, lit. "wisdom", broader than *falsafa*; scientific knowledge, including all branches of Aristotelian philosophy; occurs in *Qur'ān*; is Ibn Rushd's usual name for philosophy in *Faṣl*. Cf. Gk. *sophia*, Heb. *ḥokhmah*. See L. Gauthier, *Théorie*, pp. 46-48; Goichon.

[2] 1.7. "The purpose of this treatise": a regular opening formula in Ibn Rushd's works. Cf. *Bidāya*, p. 2; *Tahāfut*, p. 3; the six *Summaries* (*Al-jawāmiʿ aṣ-ṣighār*) of works of Aristotle, in *Rasā'il Ibn Rushd* (Hyderabad, 1947).

[3] 1.7. "the study of the Law": *an-naẓar ash-sharʿī*. *Naẓar* is theoretical study, contrasted with *ʿamal*, practice; to be translated "theory" or "study", not "speculation". Cf. Gk. *theōria*. See Goichon. For *sharʿī* see note 5.

[4] 1.8. "philosophy": *al-falsafa*, from Gk. *philosophia*; more particularly Greek and Greco-Arabic philosophy. Used less frequently than *ḥikma* in *Faṣl*. See L. Gauthier, *Théorie*, pp. 46-48; Goichon. Similarly the philosophers are less often called *falāsifa* than *ahl al-burhān*, "people of demonstration". The vocabulary is carefully chosen to give "protective colouring" to the philosophers in Islam; but the original Greek names cannot be avoided altogether if the right to philosophize is to be upheld.

"logic": *ʿulūm al-manṭiq*. This is the only mention of the word in *Faṣl*, though the science itself is discussed on pp. 2-4. Logic is not regarded as a part of philosophy: see below 2.21-3.1 and note 28.

[5] 1.8. "Law": *ash-sharʿ*, the sacred texts of Scripture regarded as sources of God's Law for Muslims; more particularly the *Qur'ān*, also the Traditions. To be translated as "Law", as a source of commands, or "Scripture", as an object of study.

[6] 1.9. The question concerning philosophy is expressed formally: in which of the legal categories (*al-aḥkām*) is it to be placed? Ibn Rushd mentions four out of the five categories: (1) obligatory

(*wājib*), (2) recommended (*mandūb*)—these two together are classed as "commanded" (*ma'mūr bihi*); (3) allowed (*mubāḥ*); and (5) prohibited (*maḥẓūr*). He does not need to mention (4) disapproved (*makrūh*), because his answer is not going to revolve around the two lower classes at all. In *Bidāya*, p. 5, Ibn Rushd gives the complete scheme, using the same terms; cf. also Ibn Khaldūn, *Muqaddima*, in *Prolégomènes*, III, p. 1. See I. Goldziher, *Ẓâhiriten* (Leiden, 1884), pp. 66-68; L. Gauthier, *Théorie*, p. 37 (but Gauthier was mistaken in regarding *maḥẓūr* as (4) and (5) together, "forbidden").

The formulation of an ethical question in terms of divine commandments does not mean that Ibn Rushd accepts such commandments as the ultimate ethical standard. Elsewhere he emphatically rejects the theistic subjectivism (ethical voluntarism) of the Ash'arites, holding that God commands an objective good: in the *Summary of Aristotle, Metaph.*, pp. 171-72 (= *Epitome*, p. 145); *Manāhij*, p. 113; *Commentary on Pl. Rep.*, I, xi, 3; *Tafsīr*, pp. 1714-15. But he regards Scripture as the main vehicle by which God makes the practical good known to most men: see *Tahāfut*, pp. 255-56, 581; *Faṣl*, pp. 18-19. This is sufficient to justify him in discussing the question of *Faṣl* in legal terms, from the standpoint of *an-naẓar ash-sha'rī*. See Introduction, pp. 18-20, for a general account of the problem of *Faṣl*.

[CHAPTER ONE]

7 1.10. Summary: Ibn Rushd commences his answer by stating, as a hypothesis, the legal syllogism required to prove his main conclusion. In the summary I have inverted the major premiss, to make it correspond more closely with what he eventually proves. The syllogism as it is actually formulated here by Ibn Rushd involves the fallacy of undistributed middle: If philosophy is a teleological study of the world, and if the Law commands a teleological study of the world, then the Law commands philosophy. Evidently philosophy might not be the kind of teleological study commanded.

Another fault in the formulation concerns the distribution of "philosophy". It is here universal, for philosophy is said to be "nothing more than" teleological study of the world; but in the eventual proof it is particular, i.e. that study is only proved to be a part of philosophy. See Introduction, p. 21, for a general criticism of this point.

8 1.10. "existing beings": *al-mawjūdāt*.

9 1.10. "as indications of . . .": *min jihat dalālatihā*. Ar. *dalīl* is Gk. *sēmeion*, which is less than demonstration; it is inductive evidence, establishing probability in proportion to its frequency. See S. Van der Bergh's notes on *Epitome*, 6.3, and *Tahāfut*, 319.6.

[10] 1.10. "the Artisan": *aṣ-ṣāni'*. The root *ṣn'* occurs several times in the same sentence, and it is necessary to reproduce the common root in translation (as Gr.). "Artisan" (Gr.) conveys a hint of Ibn Rushd's conception of God as a *dēmiourgos* (Pl. *Timaeus*), not as a Creator *ex nihilo*.

[11] 1.13. "knowledge of the Artisan": Ibn Rushd attached great value to teleological arguments for the existence and nature of God. *Manāhij*, pp. 43-46, 79: the *Qur'ān* proves the existence of God from indications of providence for man and of form and design in the world. These proofs are for all classes of men, but the learned understand the art and the Artisan more deeply. *Manāhij*, p. 84: Ibn Rushd hopes to write a book on providence. *Summary of Aristotle, Metaph.*, p. 140: Psychology leads to knowledge of God; pp. 146 ff., evidence of design in the heavenly bodies; p. 171, and in animals. *Summary of Aristotle, De physico auscultu*, pp. 16-17: Everything in nature has a purpose, as Aristotle affirms. Ibn Abī Uṣaybi'a, *'Uyūn al-anbā'*, p. 77: a saying of Ibn Rushd, "He who works at the science of anatomy increases his faith in God the Exalted." *Faṣl*, p. 4. *Tafsīr*, p. 10: "For the special Law (*sharī'a*) of the wise is to examine all beings, since the Creator can be worshipped in no nobler way than by the knowledge of His products, which leads to the knowledge of His glorious essence in its reality."

Cf. Fārābī, *K. al-fuṣūṣ*, p. 6 in *Rasā'il al-Fārābī* (Hyderabad, 1926); *Risāla fī mā yanbaghī*, etc., in Dieterici, XIV, p. 53; Ghazālī, *Munqidh*, pp. 86-87; Ibn Tūmart, *A'azz mā yuṭlab*, ed. J. D. Luciani in *Le livre de Mohammed Ibn Toumert* (Algiers, 1903), p. ٢٤, and quoted by I. Goldziher, *Z.D.M.G.*, 41 (1887), pp. 72-73; Ibn Ṭufayl, *Ḥayy*, pp. ٨٨-٩.

[12] 1.14. Summary: Ibn Rushd proceeds to prove the minor premiss very briefly, by inducing a general principle (*'illa*) from specific injunctions in the text of the *Qur'ān*. As he says, the examples are "countless", and there is no point in quoting more than a few.

[13] 2.1. "Reflect": *Qur'ān*, lix, 2. *I'tabirū*. See M. Mahdi, *Ibn Khaldūn's philosophy of history* (London, 1957), pp. 63-72, for a study of the meanings of *'abara* and its derivatives.

[14] 2.2. "the obligation": It is not clear how obligation has been proved, rather than recommendation, unless the imperative tense is understood as an order of obligation.

[15] 2.2. "intellectual and legal reasoning": *qiyās 'aqlī* and *shar'ī*. The former is theoretical or scientific, the latter is practical and starts from at least one Scriptural premiss. On *qiyās* see 2.10 and note 22.

[16] 2.3. "Have they not studied . . . ?": *Qur'ān*, viii, 185.

[17] 2.5-6. "So we made Abraham . . .": *Qur'ān*, vi, 75. The rest of the verse: "one of those who are assured."

[18] 2.6-7. "Do they not observe the camels . . . ?": *Qur'ān*, lxxxviii, 17-18. See Bayḍāwī's comments *ad loc.*, on the providential properties of the camel.

[19] 2.7. "and they give thought . . .": *Qur'ān*, iii, 191.

[20] 2.8. "in countless other verses": Cf. *Manāhij*, p. 42: "The whole of the *Qur'ān* is nothing but a summons to theoretical study (*naẓar*) and reflection."

[21] 2.8. Summary: The next three sections (2.8-6.14) aim to prove the major premiss. In the process, however, a modification is introduced which leads to a different premiss from that originally stated. See note 7.

[22] 2.10. "reasoning": *qiyās*. Both the definition of *qiyās* given here and its use in most contexts make it clear that it must be translated as "reasoning". "Syllogism" and "analogy" are too specialized, at any rate in *Faṣl*. Cf. Fārābī, *Iḥṣā' al-'ulūm*, p. 60: "The discourse (*qawl*) whose object is to verify any opinion was called by the ancients *al-qiyās*." Ibn Sīnā, *Najāt*, p. 47: "*Al-qiyās* is a discourse (*qawl*) composed of statements from which, if they are supposed, there necessarily follows another different statement, from their nature and not by accident." See Goichon. On Aristotle's variable use of the word *sullogismos* see H. W. B. Joseph, *An Introduction to logic*, 2nd ed. (Oxford, 1916), p. 249.

[23] 2.12. "the most perfect kind of study . . . reasoning": This is a further qualification of the minor premiss, which is evidently inferred from the nature of the Law: being the Law it demands the best from man. Cf. Fārābī, *Siyāsāt*, p. 16: "Wisdom (*ḥikma*) is to understand the best of things with the best science."

[24] 2.13. "demonstration": *burhān*, Gk. *apodeixis*. Aristotle, *Topica*, i, 1: Demonstration occurs when the premisses are either true and primary, i.e. believed on the strength of themselves, or derived ultimately from true and primary premisses. Cf. *Anal. Post.*, i, 2; *Eth. Nic.*, vi, 3.

[25] 2.16-17. "demonstrative . . . dialectical, rhetorical and fallacious reasoning": The classification of reasoning (*qiyās*) is derived from different passages in Aristotle's Organon: see especially *Anal. Prior*, ii, 23 and *Topica*, i, 1. The first three kinds are sound in different degrees, the fourth is not strictly "reasoning" at all. "dialectical": *jadalī*, Gk. *dialektikos*; based on probable premisses, generally accepted by well-informed people; see *Summary of Aristotle, Metaph.*, p. 6. "rhetorical": *khaṭābī*, Gk. *rhētorikos*; based on less probable premisses, accepted by the common people. "fallacious": *mughāliṭī* = "sophistical", *sufisṭānī*, Gk. *sophistikos*.

Cf. Fārābī, *Iḥṣā' al-'ulūm*, pp. 63-69; Ibn Sīnā, *K. al-ishārāt wat-tanbīhāt*, ed. J. Forget (Leiden, 1892), p. 80; Ghazālī, *Iljām* (Cairo, 1933: Munīrīya Press), pp. 53-56 = Span. tr. M. Asín Palacios,

Justo medio, pp. 406-11—a simplified but clear exposition. See L. Gauthier, *Ibn Rochd*, pp. 26-27; Goichon, s.v. *qiyās*.

[26] 2.18. "which of them are valid and which invalid": lit. "which of them are reasoning and which are not reasoning". It is strictly self-contradictory to say "which kinds of reasoning are not reasoning", but the expression is perhaps suggested by Aristotle, *Topica*, i, 1, where a similar verbal contradiction occurs.

[27] 2.14-20. "But it is preferable . . . and their kinds": With this chain of required knowledge cf. the one in *Tahāfut*, p. 205.

[28] 3.1. "as instruments have in practical activities": The conception of logic as an instrument of the sciences (*āla*, Gk. *organon*) was a commonplace. Cf. Fārābī, *Iḥṣā' al-'ulūm*, p. 54. On the pedagogical primacy of logic, see *Summary of Aristotle, Metaph.*, p. 3; *Summary of Aristotle, De physico auscultu*, p. 2 (logic to be studied in the works of Fārābī or the author's own handbook, *Al-mukhtaṣar aṣ-ṣaghīr*); *Comm. on Pl. Rep.*, II, xvi, 1 (priority of logic to mathematics).

[29] 3.2. "to acquire knowledge of the legal categories": *at-tafaqquh fil-aḥkām. fiqh* and its derivatives refer to the professional activities of Islamic lawyers. I have translated them as "law", "legal", etc. On the *aḥkām* see note 6; and L. Gauthier, "La racine arabe *ḥukm* et ses derivés", in *Homenaje*, pp. 435-54.

[30] 3.2. "legal syllogisms": *al-maqāyīs al-fiqhīya. Miqyās* is occasionally used by Ibn Rushd and I have translated it "syllogism" to distinguish it from *qiyās*. But this is a convention: it is not certain that there is any distinction of meaning. The phrase here is practically synonymous with *al-qiyās al-fiqhī* (3.6, etc.) and *al-qiyās ash-shar'-ī* (2.2, etc.). See notes 15 and 22.

[31] 3.1-3. "For just as . . . invalid": The obligation referred to is to know a second-order study, the *logic of* the reasoning used in law. There are two steps in the inference, but the first is here omitted. (1) The lawyer has to infer an obligation to use reasoning in the practice of law. How this is inferred is explained in *Bidāya*, pp. 2-4: the lawyer is commanded by Scripture to assign all acts to their categories; but Scripture directly indicates the categories of a limited number only; thus for the remainder the lawyer is obliged to have recourse to legal reasoning (*qiyās shar'ī*), which is "application of the category which is necessary for a certain thing by the Law to another thing on which it is silent", on the ground of similarity or some other common element. (*Bidāya*, p. 4.) Cf. Fārābī, *Iḥṣā' al- 'ulūm*, p. 107. On the controversy about the use of reasoning in law, see I. Goldziher, *Ẓâhiriten*, and J. Schacht, *The origins of Muhammadan jurisprudence* (Oxford, 1950). Legal reasoning was accepted in the Malikite school. It was rejected only by the Zahirites: *Bidāya*, p. 2; I. Goldziher, *Ẓâhiriten*.

(2) The inference from the necessity of practising legal reasoning to the necessity of studying its logic is evidently parallel to the argument about the logic of science in the previous paragraph.

[32] 3.3. "He who would know [God]": *al-ʿārif*, more fully expressed in 3.6, *al-ʿārif billāh*. This is another example of Islamic colouring: Ibn Rushd uses a term with Ṣūfī associations, but he refers to the philosophers, whose main occupation according to him is demonstrative, not mystical. See note 5, "philosophy"; Gr., notes 13 and 14.

[33] 3.7-10. "It cannot be objected . . . intellectual reasoning": A similar analogy is used by Ghazālī, *Iḥyā'*, I, pp. 165-67, to defend the technicalities of *kalām*: just as the sciences of tradition, exegesis and law invented technical terms as soon as they were needed for the explanation of those subjects, so it is permissible for *kalām* to invent such terms according to need.

[34] 3.11. "But most ⟨masters⟩ . . . [sacred] texts": All Muslims who accepted a Muʿtazilite, Ashʿarite, philosophical or other system of theology implicitly accepted the reasoning by which that system had been worked out (and hence would also accept the *study* of reasoning, logic).

The "gross literalists": *al-Ḥashwīya*. They are identified by A. S. Halkin, "The Hashwiyya", *Journal of the American Oriental Society*, 54 (1934), pp. 1-28, with the traditionists and the Hanbalites. The "refutation" consists in pointing out that the *Qur'ān* itself is full of reasoning on religious problems (so that by its example it sanctions such reasoning by others): see *Manāhij*, pp. 28-29. Cf. Ghazālī, *Iḥyā'*, I, p. 167, the same argument; and *Qisṭās*, pp. 160 ff., an account of syllogistic logic using examples from the *Qur'ān* (and without mention of Aristotle!).

[35] 3.15-16. "each succeeding scholar . . . might be completed": See 4.11 ff., and note 41.

[36] 3.16-19. "For it is difficult . . . intellectual reasoning": Cf. Kindī, *Kitāb al-Kindī ilal-Muʿtaṣim*, ed. A. F. Ahwānī (Cairo, 1948), pp. 79-80; and Ghazālī, *Mīzān al-ʿamal*, p. 50: the same observation about medicine.

[37] 3.20-21. "regardless of whether . . . or not": Cf. *Kitāb al-Kindī ilal-Muʿtaṣim*, p. 81; and Ghazālī, *Munqidh*, p. 103.

[38] 3.21 and 4.1. "sacrifice": *at-tadhkiya*. Not "purification", *at-tazkiya*, as Co., Gr. and Alonso: see Hourani, Note B.

[39] 4.6. "and if it is all correct . . . draw attention to that": Cf. 5.10-12; Aristotle, *De animā*, i, 2, 403b 20-23; Aristotle, *Metaph.*, α, i, 993b 12-14, and *Tafsīr*, pp. 8-10.

[40] 4.11. "from the art of demonstrative syllogisms": *min ṣināʿat al-maʿrifa bil-maqāyīs al-burhānīya*, lit. "from the art of the knowledge of demonstrative syllogisms". Logic is often called a *ṣināʿa*, Gk.

technē; and *ṣināʿa* is applied by Ibn Rushd to other studies which we call "sciences", e.g. in 4.21-5.7.

[41] 4.12. "one man after another": *wāḥid baʿd wāḥid.* Not "one topic after another", as Mr. and Alonso; (Gr.'s translation is ambiguous). *Tadāwul* means "circulation", successive handling of the same thing by different persons, not of different things by the same person. The rest of the sentence shows that Ibn Rushd is thinking of a chain of scholars in successive generations; cf. also 3.15-16. The idea was common currency among the Greek and Muslim philosophers. Aristotle, *Soph. Elench.*, 34, 183b 27-33: "those who discovered the beginnings of them [rhetoric and most other arts] advanced them in all only a little way, whereas the celebrities of today are the heirs (so to speak) of a long succession of men who have advanced them bit by bit, and so have developed them to their present form . . .". Cf. Aristotle, *Metaph.*, α, 1, 993b 1-2, and *Tafsīr*, p. 10 (a comment of approval). *Kitāb al-Kindī ilal-Muʿtaṣim*, p. 80: Our present knowledge has only been collected in successive periods. Fārābī, *De Platonis philosophia*, Ar. text, p. 20: In the ideal city divine and natural things should be studied by successive scholars; cf. p. 5. Fārābī, *Comm. on Risālat Ẓaynūn*, p. 9: a chain of masters of philosophy, Socrates—Plato—Aristotle—Zeno. Ibn Sīnā, Introd. to *Manṭiq al-mashriqīyīn*, quoted by S. Dunyā, Introd. to *Risāla Aḍḥawīya* (Cairo, 1949), p. 16: a chain, Fārābī—anonymous—Ibn Sīnā. Ibn Ṭufayl, *Ḥayy*, p. 11: Mysticism has been understood "only by one individual after another" (*al-fard baʿd al-fard*)—this exclusiveness is a further development which sometimes appears; cf. Ibn Khaldūn, *Muqaddima*, III, p. 226, = Fr. tr. III, p. 246. See L. Gauthier, Introd. to *Ḥayy*, 2nd ed., p. 127. See also L. Strauss, *Persecution*, pp. 46-55, on oral transmission of secret learning through single scholars in medieval Judaism.

[42] 4.17-18. "unless by a revelation or something resembling revelation": Too much is made of this statement by (1) Horten and (2) Alonso. (1) It does not show that revelation is regarded by Ibn Rushd as a mode of knowing which is altogether above natural human powers, as claimed by M. Horten, *Texte zu dem Streite*, p. 15. Ibn Rushd holds that revelation comes from God through the Active Intellect to prophets (*Tahāfut*, p. 516), and the prophet is a man with a remarkable imagination as well as intellect; but there is no sharp line dividing "natural" from "supernatural" knowledge. See L. Gauthier, *Théorie*, pp. 124-58; *Traité*, Introd., pp. xi-xiii; *Ibn Rochd*, pp. 38-40. (2) The statement does not show that man learns certain facts about nature through revelation as affirmed by Alonso, p. 155, n. 2. That was Ghazālī's view regarding astronomy and medicine: *Munqidh*, pp. 139-40. Cf. *Tahāfut*, p. 208, and S. Van den Bergh's note 125.2. But to Ibn Rushd such know-

ledge does not fall within the scope of the prophet's special functions. Besides, the present passage does not say that scientific knowledge by revelation actually occurs; the argument is only that *without* "a revelation or something similar" a single man certainly *cannot* learn much of a science. If someone says that something will not happen "unless a miracle occurs" we cannot infer that he believes miracles do occur in such cases.

43 4.19-20. "about 150 or 160 times": In *Tahāfut*, p. 207, he says "about 170 times". Actually about 109 times (diameters).

44 5.4. "except the West": Ibn Rushd is probably including Andalus in *al-Maghrib*. "The art of the principles of law" (*ṣināʿat uṣūl al-fiqh*) had been neglected there before the Almohad movement; the Malikite school had concentrated on applied law (*ʿilm al-furūʿ*).

45 5.12. "excusing them": Cf. Aristotle, *Soph. elench.* 34, 184b 2-8: If you find our investigation satisfactory, "there must remain for all of you, or for our students, the task of extending to us your pardon for the shortcomings of the inquiry, and for the discoveries thereof your warm thanks"; quoted with approval in *Tafsīr*, pp. 1020-21. Cf. *Kitāb al-Kindī ilal-Muʿtaṣim*, pp. 79-80. M. Horten, *Texte zu dem Streite*, p. 15, is thus wholly mistaken in attributing to Ibn Rushd's saying an Islamic meaning: namely that the ancient philosophers should be excused because they were unable to reach by natural means certain truths, which the Muslims have received from revelation.

46 5.15. "two qualities, . . . moral virtue": See 5.18-21 and note 48, on the full qualifications for understanding philosophy. The two mentioned here are the preconditions for attempting a study of it.

47 5.18. "estrangement from God the Exalted": Cf. *Tafsīr*, pp. 1135-36: the Ashʿarites blocked the gate of theoretical study, in their ignorance of true religion.

48 5.21. "these causes": The four causes of deficiency in philosophic understanding listed here may be reduced to three by grouping together unorganized study and lack of a teacher. They then constitute the reverse of the three requisites of philosophic understanding, which are referred to often by Ibn Rushd and have a long history in Greek and Muslim philosophy. The three requisites are, in sum: (1) Natural intelligence and desire for good, (2) sound morals based on good upbringing, (3) sound intellectual education.

In Plato's *Republic*, ii-vii, the formation of the philosophic rulers is described at length in these terms and in this order. Cf. also his *Epistle*, vii, 341d-344d. Aristotle in *Eth. Nic.* conceives the requirements for a satisfactory contemplative life in the same way. Cf. esp. *Eth. Nic.*, x, 9, 1179b 20-30: "Now some think that we are made good by nature, others by habituation, others by teaching." Aristotle accepts all three causes, but here stresses the second: "Nature's part evidently does not depend on us, . . .; while argument and teaching . . . are not powerful with all men, but the soul of the student must first have been cultivated by means of habits . . . For he who lives as passion directs will not hear argument that dissuades him, nor understand it if he does . . ." Also Aristotle, *Metaph.*, α, 3, 995a 6-14. Pseudo-Empedocles, quoted in M. Asín Palacios, *Ibn Masarra*, p. 193, on philosophy: "He who studies it must have a pure mind, a penetrating imagination, and little care for this world."

Fārābī, *Taḥṣīl*, pp. 44-45, gives the qualifications for being a philosopher: he refers to Pl. *Rep.*, and connects moral education with "true belief in the opinions of the religion in which he was born, clinging to the virtuous acts of his religion", etc. Cf. *Comm. on Risālat Zaynūn*, p. 9; *Siyāsāt*, pp. 46-48, on the need of a teacher. Ibn Sīnā, *Ishārāt*, pp. 222, the three requisites. Ghazālī, *Iḥyā'*, I, p. 170: "The learned man should limit his instruction in this science to those who possess three qualities: exclusive application and devotion to learning . . .", natural intelligence, and good morals and piety. Ghazālī, *Al-arba'īn fī uṣūl ad-dīn*, p. 25, quoted by S. Dunyā in Introd. to Ibn Sīnā, *Risāla Aḍḥawīya* (Cairo, 1949), pp. 6-7.

Ibn Rushd, *Faṣl* 5.15, 18.8-10. *Manāhij*, p. 42: Mortification of the passions is only of use as a condition of study and knowledge. *Comm. on Pl. Rep.*, II, iv, 6: Philosophers defective in morality will be a cause of disgrace and discredit to philosophy, "as is the case in this present time". *Tahāfut*, p. 256; pp. 361-62 gives the three qualifications for study of philosophy as natural intelligence, perseverance and leisure. *Tafsīr*, pp. 45-47, stresses the importance of a good nature and connects the classes of mind (demonstrative, etc.) with grades of natural intelligence.

Finally, two reference from thirteenth-century historians. Ibn Abī Uṣaybi'a, *'Uyūn al-anbā'*, II, p. 75: Abū Bakr Ibn Zuhr, a contemporary and friend of Ibn Rushd, refused to teach logic to two medical students in Seville until they had studied Scripture and persevered in observing its prescriptions. Marrākushī, *Mu'jib*, p. 175: When Ibn Ṭufayl proposed to Ibn Rushd the task of commenting on Aristotle, he said: " 'I expect you will be equal to it, from what I know of the excellence of your mind, the purity of your nature, and the strength of your application to science' ".

49 6.1-3. "For this manner of harm . . . by accident": Aristotle, *Soph. elench.*, 5, 166b 28-30: "Fallacies, then, that depend on Accident occur whenever any attribute is claimed to belong in a like manner to a thing and to its accident."

[50] 6.3-5. "This was the thought . . . that lied": found in Bukhārī, Muslim, *et al.*: see Wensinck, *Concordance*, I, p. 191, s.v. *baṭn*. Cf. *Qur'ān*, xvi, 69, on honey as a remedy. The point as I understand it is that the Prophet's prescription was right for typical cases, but not for accidentally abnormal ones.

[51] 6.6-7. "some of the most vicious people . . . through their study of them": Cf. Plato, *Rep.*, vi, 495b-496a, the parable of the bald tinker; Ibn Rushd, *Comm. on Pl. Rep.*, II, iv, 6, referred to in note 48.

[52] 6.12-14. "practical virtue . . . intellectual virtue": On the two kinds of virtue or excellence (*al-faḍīla*, Gk. *aretē*), see Aristotle, *Eth. Nic.*, vi, 1-2: Intellectual virtue is the best state of the scientific part of the soul, "by which we contemplate (*theōroumen*) the kind of things whose originative causes are invariable" (vi, 1139a 6-8); the good of this part is truth. Practical or moral virtue is the best state of the calculative part of the soul, "by which we contemplate variable things" (vi, 1, 1139a 8); the good of this part is "truth in agreement with right desire" (vi, 2, 1139a 30-31). Cf. also i, 13 and ii, 1. Lawyers (*al-fuqahā'*) have to possess practical virtue because jurisprudence (*al-fiqh*) consists in discovering right practice from Scripture (*Faṣl*, 19. 1-4).

[53] 6.14. Summary: The following section forms a transition between the subjects of the first two "chapters". It brings in a new point, the three methods of assent, which is important in the following chapters.

[54] 6.15. "true": *ḥaqq*. Gr. translates as "*de bon aloi*" ("genuine"), here and in 7.6. He defends this in note 21 on the ground that Scripture consists of symbols for the use of the people, which for the philosopher are not strictly true. I do not think this is a sufficient reason for not translating *ḥaqq* as "true". *Faṣl* is an exoteric work and was not meant to give away the secret thoughts of philosophers. "True" has the same ambiguity as *ḥaqq* and may embrace the notion of "genuine". But "genuine" does not cover all the meaning that Ibn Rushd meant to convey (to the public at least) by "true". This is especially clear in 7.6: " . . . this religion is *ḥaqq* and summons to the study which leads to the knowledge of the *ḥaqq*". Here the second *ḥaqq* must be "true", and the argument requires that the first *ḥaqq* should have the same meaning. Cf. also 7.8-9: "*al-ḥaqq* does not oppose *al-ḥaqq*", referring to philosophy and religion. Since philosophy is true, religion too is being called "true" in some sense (and here Gr. translates as "*verité*"). Finally it should be remembered that for Ibn Rushd Scripture contains both *ẓāhir* and *bāṭin*, and the inner meaning (*bāṭin*) is true in the literal sense. Gauthier's argument is based on an erroneous equation of Scripture with the symbolic *ẓāhir* alone.

55 6.16. "that [end]": *dhālika*, which is vague. I understand it to refer to the attainment of happiness through religion.

56 6.17-21. "For the natures of man are on different levels . . . demonstrative arguments": The three grades of intellect correspond to the three kinds of sound reasoning: see 2.16-17 and note 25. This development of Aristotelian logic was current among the Muslim philosophers. Possibly the scheme was suggested by Plato's classification of types of soul in the *Republic* (though Plato's scheme has a different basis). Cf. Fārābī, *De Platonis philosophia*, p. 22; *Comm. on Risālat Zaynūn*, p. 8; *Taḥṣīl*, pp. 36-38, 40-41. But Fārābī distinguishes only two classes: the élite, *al-khāṣṣa*, who are taught by demonstrative proofs, and the masses, *al-ʿāmma* or *al-jumhūr*, who are taught by "persuasive" and "imaginative" methods. The same two in Ibn Ḥazm, *Fiṣal*, in M. Asín Palacios, *Abenházam*, pp. 184-87. The three classes appear in Ghazālī, *Qisṭās*, pp. 188-95, with the middle class named *ahl al-jadal*; in *Munqidh*, pp. 80-83, 84, the theologians are described in terms appropriate to dialectical thinkers, but not named as such.

Ibn Rushd on the dialectical class: *Faṣl*, p. 24, they are tacitly identified with the theologians (*mutakallimūn*); *Manāhij*, pp. 56-57, they are essentially a sub-class of "the masses" (*al-jumhūr*); *Manāhij*, pp. 67-68, they have doubts but cannot solve them, they see the ambiguities in Scripture but cannot explain them, they are like sick people who cannot take the normal diet.

57 7.1-3. "except him who stubbornly . . . neglect of such matters": Cf. 15.2-4, where the same two kinds of person, the stubborn and the careless, are called unbelievers.

58 7.3. " 'the white man' ": '*al-aḥmar*', lit. " 'the red man' ", referring to the peoples of Europe, Western Asia and North Africa whom we now call white.

59 7.5-6. " 'Summon . . . by wisdom and by good preaching, and debate with them . . .' ": *Qur'ān*, xvi, 125. " 'Wisdom' " is *al-ḥikma*, a common name for philosophy, see note on 1.1, "philosophy". " 'Preaching' " is *al-mawʿiẓa*, suggesting also oratory, rhetoric, *al-khiṭāb*. " 'Debate' " is *jādil*, suggesting dialectic, *al-jadal*. Thus the quotation is neatly used to give Qur'anic sanction to the three Aristotelian types of reasoning. It is not surprising to find terms of Arabic philosophy in the *Qur'ān*: Qur'anic words were naturally chosen by Arabic theologians and philosophers in building their vocabulary. The same quotation had already been used for the same purpose by Ghazālī, *Qisṭās*, pp. 156-57, and *Iljām*, p. 59, = Span. tr. M. Asín Palacios, *Justo medio*, p. 417. There is an allusion to the three methods in the same Qur'anic words by Ibn Ṭufayl, *Ḥayy*, p. ١٥١; but Ḥayy found all three methods unavailing with most people.

[CHAPTER TWO]

[60] 7.6. Summary: The axiom contained in this important little section, that two truths cannot conflict, had been applied by Fārābī in *Jam'* to Plato and Aristotle. *Jam'*, pp. 1-3: Philosophy is knowledge of one reality; Plato and Aristotle are philosophers; therefore they must know the same reality and cannot disagrees Their apparent disagreements are explained in the remainder of *Jam'*. Cf. Ibn Ṭufayl, *Ḥayy*, pp. ١٤٤-٤٥: the harmony of Asāl'. religion and Ḥayy's philosophy.

[61] 7.9-10. "an act . . . reasoning from Scripture": Cf. *Bidāya*, pp. 2-4: The number of possible acts is infinite, while the texts of Scripture and the acts and decisions of the Legislator are finite. In cases where these sources are silent, the lawyer has to apply *qiyās shar'ī*. See note 31, on legal reasoning. The point of the parallel is simply the absence of contradiction between "unmentioned" knowledge and Scripture. The inference of legal knowledge from Scripture is, I think, referred to incidentally, since Islam does not require that all scientific knowledge should be inferred from Scripture.

[62] 7.15-18. "The meaning . . . metaphorical speech": Ibn Rushd is not thinking of mystical meanings intimately related to the words in the manner described by H. Corbin, *Avicenne et le récit visionnaire* (Teheran, 1954), II, pp. 32 ff.: see my introd., pp. 27-28. The inner meanings according to Ibn Rushd are matters of rational knowledge. And they are not allegorical fancies to be read into the text at will, but are really intended by the author of Scripture: see Alonso's note *ad loc.* Their presence can be discovered by demonstrative reasoning.

" 'allegorical interpretation' ": *'at-ta'wīl'*.

"real": *ḥaqīqīya*, equivalent to *dhātī*, "essential", in *Manāhij*, 125.16; both are used by Ghazālī, *Fayṣal*, p. 34.

"metaphorical": *majāzīya*. Here it is used in a general sense for all meanings that are not *ḥaqīqīya*; for a more specialized sense see *Manāhij*, 125.16.

Other contrasting terms used by Ibn Rushd as approximately equivalent to the above: "the apparent meaning", *aẓ-ẓāhir*, and "the inner meaning", *al-bāṭin*; "the symbol", *al-mithāl*, and "the symbolized", *al-mumaththal*.

"Arabic": The standard language by which Scripture must be interpreted was generally taken to be that of Scripture itself and that of the pre-Islamic Arabs as preserved in their poetry. But Ibn Ḥazm rejected the latter: see I. Goldziher, *Ẓâhiriten*, pp. 125-26.

[63] 7.18-20. "Now if the lawyer . . .": When can the lawyer interpret Scripture metaphorically? Not in order to harmonize it with legal knowledge from some external source, for Scripture

must prevail over any such source. But if two passages of Scripture appear to contradict each other, they must be reconciled by harmonizing interpretation. See J. Schacht, *Origins*, pp. 13 ff.

The proper treatment of Scripture in relation to legal and scientific knowledge may now be summarized in the following manner, reflecting Ibn Rushd's doctrine:

1. Legal truth unmentioned in Scripture must be inferred from it;

and scientific truth unmentioned in Scripture can sometimes be inferred from it.

2. (a) Legal statements in Scripture which harmonize with other statements in it, or scientific statements in it which harmonize with external scientific truth, must be accepted in their apparent meaning.

(b) Legal statements in Scripture which conflict with other more authoritative statements in it, or scientific statements in it which conflict with external scientific truth, must be interpreted allegorically.

64 7.20. "reasoning based on opinion": *qiyās ẓannī*. Legal reasoning had often been opposed by scholars because of its seemingly arbitrary character.

65 8.2. "doubted by no believer": Cf. Ghazālī, *Fayṣal*, pp. 85-87: All sects have used *ta'wīl*; even Ibn Ḥanbal interpreted three Traditions metaphorically, and he would have been forced to do this more often if he had been more of an intellectual. *Iḥyā'*, I, pp. 178-80: Ibn Ḥanbal was extreme in his attitude to *ta'wīl*. But Ibn Ḥazm rejected *ta'wīl* altogether.

66 8.3-4. "to reconcile the assertions of intellect and tradition": *al-jam' bayn al-ma'qūl wal-manqūl*. Cf. Ibn Ṭufayl, *Ḥayy*, p. ١٤٤; "Asāl had no doubt that all the things revealed in Scripture concerning God . . . were symbols of these things which Ḥayy Ibn Yaqẓān had seen. The eyes of his heart were opened, the fire of his thought was kindled, and the assertions of intellect and tradition fitted together in his mind (*taṭābaqa 'indahu al-ma'qūl wal-manqūl*). The methods of *ta'wīl* became accessible to him", etc.

67 8.6. "that allegorical interpretation": *dhālik at-ta'wīl*, something identical in content with "the conclusion of demonstration", really contained in the (first) "statement in Scripture", and obtainable from its apparent meaning by *ta'wīl*.

68 8.7. "the Muslims are unanimous": *ajma'a al-Muslimūn*. Ibn Rushd accepts the principle of *ijmā'* and argues on that basis in the following pages. Cf. *Manāhij*, 72.3-5, where he criticizes Ghazālī's *Fayṣal* for allowing allegorical interpretations regardless of whether they transgress *ijmā'*. As a lawyer and judge Ibn Rushd could not but admit *ijmā'*. Cf. *Bidāya*, pp. 5-6.

[69] 8.9. "the Ash'arites . . . allegorical interpretation": The followers of Ash'arī (873-935) allowed *ta'wīl* of anthropomorphic passages in Scripture. Cf. 20.20-21.1: Their interpretations are dialectical and popular, and generally less sound than those of the Mu'tazilites. 23.20-14.1: The Ash'arites used allegory less frequently than the Mu'tazilites. Cf. *Manāhij*, p. 42.

[70] 8.9. "the verse about God's directing Himself": *āyat al-istiwā'*. *Qur'ān*, ii, 29: "He it is who has created for you all that is on earth; then He directed Himself towards the heaven and made them [sic] seven heavens. He is the knower of all things." Cf. vii, 54; and xli, 11, quoted below at 13.11-12. The Ash'arites objected to the physical implications of a literal "direction" taken by God.

[71] 8.9. "the Tradition about His descent": *ḥadīth an-nuzūl*. "God descends to the heaven of the lower world", i.e. of our sublunary sphere. Wensinck, *Concordance*, s.v. *samā'*; Bukhārī, xcvii, 35, etc.

[72] 8.9-10. "the Hanbalites take them in their apparent meaning": They did not interpret them physically, but simply refused to interpret them at all, accepting the literal meaning without seeking an explanation (*bilā kayfa*). The traditionist Tirmidhī (d. A.D. 892), when asked for an explanation of this verse, replied: " 'Descent' is understood, but the manner is unknown; faith in it is obligatory, questions about it are heresy": Ibn Khallikān, *Wafayāt al-a'yān*, ed. Wüstenfeld, No. 583, p. 103.

[73] 8.11-12. "The reason why . . . which reconciles them": Cf. Ibn Sīnā, *Najāt*, p. 500, on the duties of a prophet: "And there is no harm if his discourse includes enigmas and hints, to summon those naturally qualified for theoretical study to philosophic research about religious observances and their utility in this life and the next."

"which reconciles them": *al-jāmi' baynahā*; "them" refers to the apparent contradictions.

[74] 8.13-14. " 'He it is . . . well grounded in science' ": *Qur'ān*, iii, 7. The relevant parts of the verse are 'other [verses] are ambiguous . . . No one knows their interpretation except God and those who are well grounded in science'. See 10.6-9 and note 87, on Ibn Rushd's interpretation of this verse; see that note for the full quotation. He assumes, quite safely, that his readers know the verse. See Gr., n. 25. Ibn Rushd's belief that the contradictions in Scripture are deliberate lacks any historical or critical basis: see Alonso, p. 164, n. 4.

[75] 8.14-16. "It may be objected: ' . . . they have disagreed' ": The threefold division of texts of Scripture in this passage corresponds roughly and superficially to the threefold division elaborated in 14.12-16.19. But the bases of the divisions are different: here it is

ijmā', there it is an objective character of the texts themselves. And here, though Ibn Rushd admits the principle of *ijmā'*, he does not admit that it ever applies in fact to texts on dogma; whereas in the later passage he is working out a theory of his own, which he thinks is really applicable to such texts.

76 8.18. "Abū Ḥāmid": Ghazālī (1059-1111). Nine works of Ghazālī are referred to by Ibn Rushd in *Manāhij*, pp. 69-72: see Alonso, p. 166, n. 1. Others in *Tahāfut*: see S. van den Bergh, Index to Notes.

77 "Abul-Ma'ālī": Juwaynī (1028-85), Ash'arite theologian, known as Imām al-Ḥaramayn; Ghazālī's teacher at Nīshāpūr. Ibn Rushd refers to his *Niẓāmīya* (*Manāhij*, p. 38), and his *Irshād* (*Manāhij*, p. 76).

78 8.20. "in matters like these"; i.e. matters of theory or belief, not matters of practices or morals. For Ghazālī's view see *Fayṣal*, pp. 87-95.

79 9.4. "unassailable authority": *naql tawātur*. This is defined by Najm ad-dīn an-Naṣafī (d. 1142) as "the narrative established by the tongues of people of whom it is inconceivable that they would agree together on a falsehood. It brings about necessary knowledge such as the knowledge of former kings in past times and of distant countries": Eng. tr. E. Elder in *A commentary on the creed of Islam* (New York, 1950), p. 15. See Goichon, s.v. *tawāturī*, *mutawātirāt*.

80 9.10-11. " 'Speak to people . . . lying' ": Wensinck, *Concordance*, s.v. *ḥaddatha*; Bukhārī, iii, 49.

81 9.11. "early believers": *as-salaf*. Cf. Ibn Ṭufayl, *Ḥayy*, p. ١٠٠: In revealing hidden science "we have abandoned the way of the good early believers" who were sparing in this matter.

82 9.14-16. "The situation is different . . . handed down to us": This negative rule for establishing *ijmā'* was no doubt necessary if the law was to make any use of the principle. But even in practical matters a stricter, positive rule was demanded by opponents of *ijmā'*. E.g. Shāfi'ī, as summarized by Schacht: "The consensus of the majority of those scholars on whom one happens to possess information cannot be used as an argument, and no inference may be drawn regarding the opinion of those scholars of whom nothing is known": J. Schacht, *Origins*, p. 92. Others opposed *ijmā'* because it is impossible to know all who were qualified *mujtahids*, or whether they all agreed that it is permissible to give out their opinions: Juwaynī, *Waraqāt*, fol. 33b, in I. Goldziher, *Ẓâhiriten*, p. 33. But the lawyers' objections to *ijmā'* sprang from a desire to restrict the sources of law as far as possible to the *Qur'ān* and the *sunna* of the Prophet, whereas Ibn Rushd's objections are inspired by the aim of permitting latitude to philosophers.

83 9.19. "Abū Naṣr": Fārābī (d. 950).

84 9.19. "Ibn Sīnā": Avicenna (980-1037).

85 9.20. "*The disintegration*": *At-tahāfut*, i.e. *Tahāfut al-falāsifa*, "*The disintegration of the philosophers*", completed in Baghdād, 1095. For discussions of the meaning of *tahāfut* see L. Gauthier, *Théorie*, p. 99, n. 1; M. Bouyges, Introd. to *Tahāfut al-falāsifa* (Beirut, 1927), pp. x-xi; L. Gardet, "Raison et foi en Islam", *Revue Thomiste*, 43 (1937), pp. 437-78, and 44 (1938), pp. 145-67, 342-78.

86 10.1-3. "We answer . . . can only be tentative": Ibn Rushd's answer at this point is that Ghazālī could not have meant what he said in *Tahāfut al-falāsifa*, because his assertion there is overruled by his more general statement in *Fayṣal*, pp. 87-89 (see above, 8.20 and note). But this cannot be correct, for in *Fayṣal* too he says that the philosophers' views on two of the three questions must be condemned as unbelief: pp. 90-91. The explanation seems to be that Ghazālī does condemn them *but not on grounds of ijmāʿ*. (Ibn Rushd should have seen this, since in *Manāhij*, p. 72, he criticizes Ghazālī for admitting that *ta'wīl* could be acceptable even if it violates *ijmāʿ*). Ghazālī's condemnation of the philosophic doctrines has a more objective basis: his theory of interpretation, worked out in *Fayṣal*, pp. 80 ff. Its general principle is that Scripture must not be understood metaphorically if it can be understood in a more literal sense. See Alonso, p. 170, n. 1.

"*The distinction*": *Fayṣal*, i.e. *K. fayṣal at-tafriqa bayn al-Islām waz-zandaqa*, "The book of the decisive distinction between Islam and heathenism", written some years after Ghazālī's departure from Baghdād in 1095.

"tentative": *fīhi iḥtimāl*. Lane gives *muḥtamal* as "possible". Ibn Rushd in *Bidāya*, pp. 3-4, contrasts *muḥtamal* with *ẓāhir*, as that which is less clearly indicated by a text.

87 10.6-9. "These are 'those who are well grounded . . .' among the unlearned": *Qur'ān*, iii, 7. The verse in full can be rendered as follows (I omit punctuation at the point of ambiguity). 'He it is who has sent down to you the Book, containing certain verses clear and definite—they are the essence of the Book—and others ambiguous. Now those in whose hearts is mischief go after the ambiguous passages, seeking discord and seeking to interpret them allegorically. But no one knows their interpretation *except God and those who are well grounded in science they say* "We believe in it, it is all from our Lord; but only men of intelligence give heed" '.

The italicized words may be punctuated in two ways: (1) The full stop may be placed after 'God'; thus the learned are *excluded* from those who know the allegorical interpretations. The attitude of the learned to those verses is then one of belief and heeding, while at the same time they recognize their inability to understand them. (2) The stop may be put after 'science'; thus the learned are *included* in those who know the allegorical interpretations. Their attitude is then to *say* no more than that they believe in them, while hinting in the last sentence that men of intelligence understand them.

Ibn Rushd prefers (2), but the reason he gives here is not very convincing: that the superiority in the belief of the learned consists in their knowing the interpretations demonstratively. Apart from the anachronism of finding Greek logical concepts in the *Qur'ān*, there is another explanation which seems more in accord with its spirit: the belief of the learned is superior to that of the mischief-makers because the former humbly recognize the limits of their own understanding and the obligation to believe without going into the ambiguous verses. This explanation implies (1). But (1) is sounder for several reasons of sense and grammar. See L. Gauthier, *Théorie*, pp. 59-68; *Traité*, n. 25.

Other references to this verse in *Faṣl*: 8.13-14; 16.12-13 and 21.16-19, where Ibn Rushd recommends (1) for popular consumption. *Manāhij*, 125.3-4, 126-15.

88 10.10. "this [belief]": i.e. "the belief which is based on demonstration". Ar. *hādhā* alone, which is ambiguous; but I do not think it can refer to "demonstration" (as Gr. tr. "celle-çi", Alonso, "la cual"), because demonstration as such is not limited to interpretation of Scripture. The Escurial MS. has a marginal gloss *īmān* ("belief").

89 10.9-11. "God has described . . . allegorical interpretation": This sentence expands the argument of the last; it connects a superior belief with allegorical interpretation by the link of demonstrative reasoning. Superior belief must be based on demonstration, and the only *relevant* use of demonstration is in determining allegorical interpretations.

For Ibn Rushd's identification of the "men of sound learning" mentioned in the *Qur'ān* with the "demonstrative scholars", cf. *Manāhij*, 39.20-21 and 54.6-7. The former passage is criticized by Ibn Taymīya, *Al-jam' bayn al-'aql wan-naql* in *Falsafat Ibn Rushd* (Cairo, no date, Raḥmānīya Press), p. 133.

90 10.12-13. "and if this belief . . . interpretation": a repetition of the preceding argument, in 10.9-11.

91 10.14. "those [verses] have": *lahā*. The reference must be to "the ambiguous verses", *mutashābihāt*, in *Qur'ān*, iii, 7. This antecedent has not been quoted in the text but would be in the minds of readers.

92 10.16. "general unanimity": *ijmā' mustafīḍ*. *Mustafīḍ* is lit. "widespread", "broadcast". See Gr., n. 32.

93 10.17. Summary: On the question of God's knowledge of particulars, and on the other two philosophical questions, Ibn

Rushd in *Faṣl* says just enough to refute Ghazālī's charges of irreligion against the philosophers. I shall follow his example in the notes on these questions, and not attempt a commentary on the philosophical points at issue. Ibn Rushd's doctrine on God's knowledge of particulars is explained more fully in *Tahāfut*, pp. 455-68, answering Ghazālī point by point; *Ḍamīma; Summary of Aristotle, Metaph.*, pp. 152-53; *Tafsīr*, pp. 1706-8; *Manāhij*, pp. 51-52. Cf. Ben Maymōn, *Guide*, Part 3, chs. 16, 20-21.

94 10.17-18. "In addition to all this . . . does not know particulars at all": Ghazālī's attack on the philosophers is in *Tahāfut al-falāsifa*, 13th discussion, pp. 223-38. See Alonso, p. 172, n. 1, on Ghazālī's own view of God's knowledge.

95 11.3-4. "many names . . . light and darkness": Such polarity of meaning is recorded frequently in the dictionaries of classical Arabic. See Gr., n. 34.

96 11.6. "We have devoted . . . one of our friends": The reference is to *Ḍamīma*. See notes 198 and 199.

97 11.8. "true visions": *ar-ru'yā aṣ-ṣādiqa*, lit. "the true vision"; but I have avoided the sing. "vision" which has another meaning, "insight".

98 11.6-10. "But how can anyone imagine . . . rules the universe?": Cf. *Ḍamīma*, 131.11-13. This view is not supported by Aristotle, *De divinatione per somnum*: It is unlikely that God is the cause of premonitions in dreams, because they occur to inferior persons more often than to the wisest and best (1, 462b, 20-22 and 2, 464c 19-24). Further, "On the whole, . . . it may be concluded that dreams are not sent by God", for they occur to some of the lower animals (2, 463b, 11-15).

99 11.15. Summary. The philosophical question, whether the world was eternal in the past (*qadīm*) or originated (*muḥdath*) at a finite past time aroused great interest in the medieval Arabic world. See esp. Fārābī, *Jam'*, pp. 22-25; Ghazālī, *Tahāfut al-falāsifa*; Ibn Rushd, *Tahāfut; Manāhij*, pp. 79-92; Ben Maymōn, *Guide*, Part 1, chs. 69, 71, 74, 75, Part 2, chs. 2, 13-22, 25. Abū Ya'qūb asked Ibn Rushd about the opinion of the philosophers on this question, at the interview: Marrākushī, *Mu'jib*, p. 174. The first question of the Emperor Frederick II to Ibn Sab'īn was about Aristotle's doctrine of the eternity of the world: *Al-masā'il aṣ-Siqilīya*, extracts ed. M. Amari, "Questions philosophiques adressés aux savants musulmans par l'empereur Fréderic II", *Journal Asiatique*, 5th Series, 1 (1853), pp. 240-74.

On the particular topic discussed here, the comparison of philosophic and Ash'arite doctrines of the world, Ibn Rushd wrote a special treatise, described by Ibn Abī Uṣaybi'a as showing "that the doctrines of the Peripatetics and of the Muslim theologians on the manner of existence of the world are close to each other": '*Uyūn al-anbā'*, II, pp. 77-78. This treatise exists in a medieval Hebrew translation: ed. M. Worms, *Die Lehre von der Anfangslosigkeite der Welt* (Münster, 1900), pp. 66-70. Its argument agrees with this passage of *Faṣl*. Cf. also *Tahāfut*, p. 124.

[100] 12.5. "the Maker": *al-fā'il*. Or "the Agent". Cf. 11.20, "an efficient cause", *sabab fā'il*; 12.8, "an agent", *fā'il*.

[101] 12.13. "that it": *annahu*, referring directly to past being; but also to past time, whose finitude is dependent on that of being, see 12.10-11.

[102] Ibn Rushd's understanding of Pl. *Timaeus* is probably incorrect: see F. M. Cornford, *Plato's cosmology* (London, 1937), pp. 24-26. He is following Fārābī, *Jam'*, p. 22. Ghazālī knew the view of some Greek commentators that Plato did not believe in the temporal beginning of the world or the finitude of time: *Tahāfut al-falāsifa*, p. 21.

[103] 12.15. "generated": *kā'in*. Cf. *al-kawn wal-fasād*, "generation and corruption". On the meanings of *kāna* see A.-M. Goichon, *La philosophie d'Avicenne et son influence en Europe medievale* (Paris, 1944), pp. 61 ff.; and *Lexique*, s.v. *kawn*.

[104] 12.20. " 'coeval with time' ": *azalīyan*, Gk. *agenēton*; the general words for that which is never transformed so long as it exists, in past, present, or future, in contrast with things which arise out of something else and are dissolved into something else. But it may be conceived as brought into existence by an agent, though not out of any pre-existing matter.

[105] 13.1-3. "contraries such as the theologians suppose . . . not the case": Ibn Rushd means that "pre-eternity" (*qidam*) and "coming into existence" (*ḥudūth*) in their *loose* sense, as they are commonly applied to the world, are not contraries. In their *strict* sense, as defined above in [1] and [2], the two terms are contraries.

[106] 13.4. "these opinions": i.e. those of the theologians about the creation of the world.

[107] 13.5-6. "its *form* really is originated": The form of the world is *muḥdatha* in approximately the sense defined above, 11.20-12.3: it is brought into existence by an efficient cause and out of something else (a previous form, not matter). According to this view the Creation of the world described in Scripture consisted in its being given its present form, not its being brought into existence as matter—it already existed as matter but in another form. Cf. *Tahāfut*, p. 396.

[108] 13.7-8. " 'He it is . . . on the water' ": *Qur'ān*, xi, 7. The anterior existence of matter, which Ibn Rushd noticed in the Qur'anic accounts of the Creation, can also be seen in Genesis, i. See L. Gauthier, *Ibn Rochd*, p. 198.

[109] 13.10. " 'On the day .. and the heavens as well' ": *Qur'ān*, xiv, 48.

[110] 13.11-12. " 'Then He directed Himself . . . smoke' ": *Qur'ān*, xli, 11. Cf. *Qur'ān*, ii, 29, and vii, 54.

[111] 13.15-16. "Then how is it conceivable . . . by a school of philosophers!": Ibn Rushd implies that the philosophers (*al-ḥukamā'*) of Islam are among the learned whose assent is required to establish *ijmā'*.

[112] 13.17. Summary: There follows in 13.17-16.19 what appears at first sight to be a long digression on excusable and inexcusable error. In reality this doctrine of error provides an elaborate foundation for the answer to the third charge against the philosophers, taken up at 16.19.

[113] 13.17-18. "It seems . . . in error": The question that has just been discussed was whether to interpret allegorically the verses of the *Qur'ān* about the Creation. Because of the difficulty of deciding the question, these texts fall into class [iii] described below, 16.15-19, on which disagreement among scholars is to be expected and error by anyone of them is excusable.

The "merit" and "excuse" referred to are obtainable at the balancing of accounts on the Day of Judgement. The discussion now moves from the plane of *ijmā'* to a more objective level, where the rightness of beliefs is determined by the care with which judgement is exercised, within the limits of each man's capacity and qualifications. The excusing of error by scholars is in line with the well-known Tradition quoted below at 14.1-2, as well as with Aristotelian sentiment; cf. 5.12 and note 45.

[114] 13.18-20. "For assent to a thing . . . or not to stand up": It is clear enough that this doctrine has an Aristotelian source, but less clear what precisely that source is. H. A. Wolfson has linked it to Aristotle's doctrine of *pistis*, "faith" or "judgement of truth", as a function of the theoretical intellect: hence it cannot depend on free choice which is "the result of the cooperation of practical intellect with desire". He refers to *Eth. Nic.*, vi, 2, 1139a 21-26, and *De animā*, iii, 10, 433a 22-25: in "The double faith theory in Clement, Saadia, Averroes and St. Thomas, and its origin in Aristotle and the Stoics", *Jewish Quarterly Review*, N.S. 33 (1942-43), pp. 213-64, esp. pp. 215-18. The doctrine might also be considered as a development of what Aristotle says about involuntary ignorance in *Eth. Nic.*, iii, 1 and 5; but it involves a considerable extension of Aristotle's theory at this point.

[115] 13.20. "free choice is a condition of obligation": Aristotle, *Eth. Nic.*, iii, 1-5. *Qur'ān*, ii, 233, and other passages: God does not require of anyone what is beyond his capacity. See "*Taklīf*", *Encyclopaedia of Islam*, 1st ed. (Leiden, 1913-38).

[116] 14.1-2. " 'If the judge . . . a single reward' ": References in Wensinck, *Concordance*, s.v. *ijtahada*; Bukhārī, 96, 21, etc. The right to exercise personal judgement (*ijtihād*) in law was limited by Shāfiʿī to cases not explicitly decided by the *Qur'ān*, the Traditions or *ijmāʿ*. In such cases, "scholars must exert their own judgement in search of an indication (*shubha*) in one of these three sources; he who is qualified for this research is entitled to hold the opinion which he finds implied in *Koran*, *sunna*, or consensus; if a problem is capable of two solutions, either opinion may be held as the result of systematic reasoning, but this occurs only rarely": Shāfiʿī, *K. al-umm* (Cairo, 1903-7), VII, p. 261, Eng. tr. J. Schacht, *Origins*, p. 97.

[117] 14.2-5. "And what judge . . . obliges them to study": On the extension of the doctrine of *ijtihād* from legal to philosophic judgements, and its combination with Greek theories of the will, see L. Gauthier, *Théorie*, p. 104. The "judgement" of both judge and scholar is called *ḥukm*: see L. Gauthier, "La racine arabe *ḥukm* et ses derivés", in *Homenaje*, pp. 435-54. The extension of *ijtihād* to matters of belief is supported by Ghazālī, *Fayṣal*, p. 79, where he says: If you claim to follow reason you cannot at the same time condemn as unbelievers others, who follow their reasons, for reaching different conclusions. The justification implied seems the same as Ibn Rushd's: that we cannot help following our reasons. Ibn Ḥazm applies the Tradition on rewards to matters of belief: *Fiṣal*, in M. Asín Palacios, *Abenházam*, V, pp. 314 ff.

[118] 14.12. "the way to draw inferences from them": So, since the *mutakallimūn* have not studied Aristotelian logic, they are not entitled to practise *ijtihād* in matters of doctrine!

[119] 14.12. Summary: The section which follows elaborates the theory of excusable error propounded in the last section, by setting up some definite rules for interpretation of Scripture. Certain kinds of interpretation are said to be inexcusable and unbelief. Do such statements contradict those of pp. 8-10, that *ijmāʿ* can never establish any interpretations in matters of dogma as unbelief? No, because here we have a theory set up *on grounds other than ijmāʿ*. The rules for interpretation are objective and demonstrable, and anyone who transgresses them is guilty of sin or unbelief regardless of what the scholars of the past have declared. Needless to say, the Muslim philosophers had no chance of imposing this "scientific" system on society, and this is fortunate in view of its possibilities of intellectual tyranny far surpassing those of *ijmāʿ*.

[120] 14.13. "of two types": Ibn Rushd's classifying numbers in this section are somewhat misleading, and I have inserted my own numbers to make plain his real classification. The first type mentioned here concerns texts on which error is excused (14.3-16).

The second type, those on which error is not excused (14.16-17), is then subdivided into two classes, in 14.17-16.15. Consequently, when the first type is spoken of again in 16.15 it is called "a third class".

121 14.14-15. "the skilful doctor . . . the skilful judge": Analogies with medicine and law occurred readily to Ibn Rushd, both from his readings in Plato and Ghazālī and from his own professional experience. *Faṣl* contains several examples of both.

122 14.17. "unbelief": *kufr*, involving expulsion from the Islamic community; sometimes translated "infidelity", but the word has some misleading associations.

123 14.17. "heresy": *bid'a*, lit., "innovation", not involving expulsion from Islam.

124 14.18. "the methods of indication": *ṭuruq ad-dalā'il*. On *dalīl* as "indication" see note 9. These "methods of indication" in Scripture are the same as its three "methods of summons" (*ṭuruq ad-du'ā'*) mentioned in 6.17-7.6: they are the three types of argument, demonstrative, dialectical and rhetorical. As in the cases under consideration Scripture provides indications suitable for every type of mind, no one has the excuse of inability to understand.

125 15.11. "images and likenesses of these things": *amthālahā wa ashbāhahā*. *Amthāl* is pl. of *mathal*. It does not here have a technical meaning, translating Gk. *gnōmē*, "maxim", as claimed by H. A. Wolfson, "The double faith theory", *Jewish Quarterly Review*, N.S. 33 (1942-43), pp. 246-47. It can only refer to a symbol of some kind, for it is used in relation with an object, e.g. *amthālahā* (15.11), *tilk al-amthāl al-maḍrūba li tilk al-ma'ānī* (15.14). Similar remarks apply to *ashbāh*, pl. of *shibh*.

126 15.12. "the indications common to all men": *al-adilla al-mushtaraka lil-jamī'*. A good example of a "common" argument in the *Qur'ān* occurs in *Manāhij*, p. 122: the corporeal symbolization of the future life.

Cf. Fārābī, *Siyāsāt*, p. 55, on the principles of philosophy: "But most people do not have the ability either by nature or by habit to understand and conceive those things. Thus they must have the principles of things and their grades, the Active Intellect and the prime government imaged to them by things which correspond to them." Cf. Ibn Ṭufayl, *Ḥayy*, pp. ١٣٦, ١٤٤, ١٤٦-٤٧; Ben Maymōn, *Guide*, Introduction.

127 15.15-16. "These . . . *the distinction*": "These" refers to "those ideas", *tilk al-ma'ānī*. Ghazālī, *Fayṣal*, pp. 80-85: There are five modes of existence. (1) Essential, *dhātī*, or real, *ḥaqīqī*: objective existence in the real world, e.g. of the seven heavens. (2) Sensible, *ḥissī*: existing in the sense faculty only, as in dreams, visions and illusions, e.g. "Death comes as a speckled ram on the Day of

Judgement" (Tradition). (3) Imaginary, *khayālī*: "the form of these sensible things when they are absent from sense" (p. 82), e.g. in the Tradition that the Prophet was "as if seeing Jonah". (4) Intellectual, *ʿaqlī*: of things representing abstract concepts, e.g., when God formed Adam with His hand, this "hand" is God's power of grasping. (5) Metaphorical, *Shibhī*: when the thing itself does not exist in any of the other four senses, but something else exists resembling it in some respect. E.g. God's "anger": He does not have anger, but some other attribute which produces the same kind of effects as human anger, such as pain in other persons.

Cf. *Manāhij*, 125.15 ff., giving the five names and endorsing Ghazālī's doctrine. Why does Ibn Rushd hesitate here and say "four or five"? Possibly because there are four kinds of beings which can constitute an inner meaning, and one more which is the apparent meaning.

Alonso, p. 181, n. 2, infers from certain statements in *Fayṣal* that *ta'wīl* for Ghazālī embraces the interpretation of a text in the first or "essential" sense, and thus means "hermeneutic" in general and is not restricted to allegorical interpretation. However this may be in Ghazālī, it is certainly not the use of Ibn Rushd. *Mu'awwal* is regularly contrasted with *ẓāhir* (the "essential" sense); and see the explicit definition of *ta'wīl* in 7.15-18.

[128] 15.17-18. "we do not need . . . allegorical interpretation": Ibn Rushd's prohibition is based on the principle expounded by Ghazālī in *Fayṣal*, pp. 87-89: "There is no permission to turn away from one level to the next below it, without a necessary proof" (p. 87). I.e. permission to use *ta'wīl* must be based on a proof of the impossibility of a more apparent sense, beginning with "essential" existence and proceeding in order down the list of the five kinds of existence.

[129] 15.19-21. "anyone who thinks . . . his sensible existence": Cf. *Comm. on Pl. Rep.*, II, vi, 2: "Some people are of the opinion that the human end is merely to guard and preserve the body and to protect the senses." Ibn Ṭufayl, *Ḥayy*, pp. ١٥٢-٥٣: Ḥayy thought that for the masses the only benefit of the Law was to secure them in their properties in this world, that their only concern is with sensible things (*al-umūr al-maḥsūsa*), and that the Law is perfectly suited to this purpose.

[130] 16.2. "on fundamentals . . . heresy": Cf. Ghazālī, *Fayṣal*, pp. 87, 89-91.

[131] 16.3-4. "for such men . . . heresy on their part": Cf. Ghazālī, *Fayṣal*, p. 88. The doctrine is modified somewhat in 20.18-21.1, where a certain amount of allegorical interpretation is permitted to the dialectical class, Ashʿarites and Muʿtazilites.

[132] 16.5. "Of this [latter] class . . . His descent": Cf. 8.9-10 and

notes 69-72. According to the present doctrine the Ash'arites would be heretical for interpreting these texts allegorically; but see 20.18-21.1.

[133] 16.6. " 'Free her . . . believer' ": See Wensinck, *Concordance*, s.v. *samā*'; Muslim, *Masājid*, 33, etc.

[134] 16.7-10. "the class of people . . . imaginable thing": Cf. *Tafsīr*, p. 47: Those who want poetic evidence for truth are those who are unable to believe what they cannot imagine.

[135] 16.10. "the relation stated": *hādhihi an-nisba*. I.e. the relation of God to the sky.

[136] 16,11. "advanced": *shadaw*. Mr. tr., p. 15, n. 5: *shadw* means to gain a superficial knowledge of a science; quotations from Maqrīzī, Ben Maymōn, Fārābī. R. Dozy, *Supplément aux dictionnaires arabes* (Leiden, 1881) gives *shadw fī* as "être versé dans une science", with examples from Ibn Khaldūn, *Muqaddima*.

[137] 16.11. "⟨by rejecting⟩ belief in corporeality": The text should contain *bi-inkār* or another word for denial; see Hourani, *ad loc*. This is necessary to sense. The whole passage is best explained by Fārābī, *Jam'*, p. 26: He is speaking about the suitability of different expressions of truth for different levels of understanding. The man who can only understand corporeal expressions is excused and correct in doing so; if he is told more his error increases. If he can understand that God is incorporeal and creates without movement, he still may not see how He can be without a place. Cf. Ghazālī, *Fayṣal*, p. 87: The Hanbalites say there is no proof that God cannot be called "above".

[138] 16.11-13. "Thus the [proper] answer . . . 'except God' ": *Qur'ān*, iii, 7. The same answer in 21.16-19. But contrast 10.6-9: Ibn Rushd's real opinion about this verse is different; see note *ad loc*. Cf. Ben Maymōn, *Guide*, Part 1, ch. 35, Eng. tr. M. Friedländer, 2nd ed., p. 50: Those who cannot understand the true meaning of difficult passages in the prophets "may simply be told that the scriptural passage is clearly understood by the wise, but that they should content themselves with knowing that God is incorporeal". (Ben Maymōn's position is that the fact of God's incorporeality should at least be made known to all, regardless of whether it is understood.)

[139] 16.19. Summary: Whereas on the other two doctrines of the philosophers Ibn Rushd has given a brief exposition of their opinions, on the future life he gives none; he is content to establish the philosophers' right to interpret it in an incorporeal sense. *Manāhij*, pp. 122-24, discusses three positions on the future life. In both passages Ibn Rushd shows caution on the subject; the "demonstrative" view on it was obviously not one to be set down in public writings. See note on *Manāhij*, 122.17-20; Gr., n. 54.

[140] 17.5. "the two interpretations of the passages": *at-ta'wīlayn*, lit. "the two allegorical interpretations"; I omit "allegorical" in some places where the repetition seems tedious. The two allegorical interpretations are given in *Manāhij*, pp. 122-23: Some accept a purely spiritual resurrection, others a resurrection in bodies of another kind than our present ones.

[141] 17.9-10. "only the negation . . . 'the black man' ": As stated above, pp. 6-7 and 14-15, Scripture provides arguments convincing to every type of mind, i.e. demonstrative, dialectical and rhetorical arguments. These are "the three methods", and they are called "common", *mushtaraka*, here simply to indicate that *between them* they are serviceable to men of every class and condition. The adjective is confusing, because it has previously (15.12) been used in a more technical sense, to describe the dialectical and rhetorical methods: these are "common" because they can be understood by everyone, in contrast with the demonstrative method.

For the doctrine, cf. *Tahāfut*, pp. 582-86.

[142] 17.16. Summary: The following section forms a transition to Chapter 3, bringing in the prohibition of teaching philosophical allegories to the masses. There is an impressive tradition of secrecy among philosophers preceding Ibn Rushd. A complete account of the esoteric tradition would fill a book. A few references within Ibn Rushd's range of reading will suffice here.

Plato, *Epistle*, vii, 341d-344d: "I do not, however, think the attempt to tell mankind of these matters a good thing, except in the case of some few who are capable of discovering the truth for themselves with a little guidance" (341d-e). Plato's reasons were that language never expresses reality precisely as it is, and that the attempt to do so merely arouses contempt or vain hopes among those who lack the capacity to understand.

Galen, in Ibn Abī Uṣaybiʿa, *'Uyūn al-anbā'*, II, p. 96: "My discourse in this book is not for all people; my discourse is for a man among them who is equal to thousands of men, or rather tens of thousands. For the truth is not such as to be grasped by many people, but it is such as to be grasped by the excellent mind among them."

Fārābī, *Compendium legum*, ed. F. Gabrieli in *Plato Arabus*, III (London, 1952), p. 4: Plato's use of symbols and enigmas, endorsed by Fārābī. *Jamʿ*, pp. 5-7: Plato and Aristotle used different methods but had the same purpose of concealment; there is much abbreviation and omission in Aristotle's scientific works, and this is deliberate. Cf. *Risāla* in Dieterici, XIV, pp. 53-54. *Jamʿ*, p. 26: Different expressions of truth suit different levels of understanding. *Comm. on Risālat Ẓaynūn*, p. 8: Zeno said: "My teacher Aristotle reported a saying of his teacher Plato: 'The summit of knowledge is too lofty for every bird to fly to'."

Ibn Sīnā, *Najāt*, pp. 499-500: The prophet has to teach the people by symbols and enigmas; if he taught them metaphysical truths he would impose a great strain on them and overthrow their religion. *Ishārāt*, p. 222: I have given you the cream of wisdom. Preserve it from those who would waste it, etc.

Ghazālī, *Iljām* (Cairo, 1933), Span. tr. in M. Asín Palacios, *Justo medio*: an elaborate theory restricting the teaching of allegorical interpretations of Scripture to the masses. *Mīzān al-'amal*, pp. 169-77, 212-16: the duty of maintaining reserve in speaking of religion according to the understanding of hearers. *Iḥyā'*, I, pp. 161-71: restrictions on *kalām*; pp. 174-78: five kinds of secrets which should not be broadcast. *Fayṣal*, p. 88. *Al-iqtiṣād fīl-i'tiqād* (Cairo, no date, Ḥusayn Commercial Library), pp. 6-8.

Ibn Ṭufayl, *Ḥayy*, pp. ١٥٠-٥٤: uselessness of teaching the inner meaning of Scripture to the masses.

Ben Maymōn, *Guide*, Introduction, and Part 1, chs. 33-34.

Tahāfut, pp. 356-58, 361-62, 396, 463, 557: on the need for restricting philosophic studies.

On Ibn Rushd's historical environment and some general considerations, see my introduction; L. Gauthier, *Théorie*, ch. 3; and L. Strauss, *Persecution*.

On enigmatic teaching see note 191.

143 17.17-18. "as Abū Ḥāmid does": It is hard to estimate the justice of this charge against Ghazālī without a survey of all his writings and a classification of them as "demonstrative" or otherwise. The allegorical interpretations used to illustrate his theories in books like *Fayṣal* and *Qisṭās* do not appear to be dealt with by the weaker methods. Is *Mishkāt al-anwār* counted as "non-demonstrative" by Ibn Rushd?

144 17.21. "to reconcile the [first] two [groups]": *al-jam' baynahumā*. I.e. to reconcile the slanderers of philosophy and religion; not to unite slander of philosophy with slander of religion, as Alonso interprets, p. 180. Apart from the normal meaning of *jam'*, the next sentence says that "this" was one of Ghazālī's objects, and Ibn Rushd would never have accused him of wishing to slander philosophy and religion, a fantastic accusation.

Cf. *Manāhij*, pp. 70-72, for Ibn Rushd's more detailed explanation of the harm done by Ghazālī.

145 18.4. " . . . an 'Adnānī' ": The verse is by 'Imrān Ibn Ḥiṭṭān: see Mubarrad, *Kāmil*, ed. W. Wright (Leipzig, 1864-92), p. 532. Mr. tr., p. 17, n. 4.

The supposed inconsistency of Ghazālī made a strong impression on the philosophers of western Islam. Cf. *Manāhij*, p. 70, and Ibn Ṭufayl, *Ḥayy*, pp. ١٥-١٨, for some specific criticisms. The criticisms are not altogether fair, since they take no account of Ghazālī's development, his distinction between esoteric and public writings, the possibility of spurious additions to his books, or the possibility that his meaning has not been fully understood. And Ibn Rushd's criticism here is definitely unfair: there was no direct contradiction between being an Ash'arite and being a Ṣūfī, and Ghazālī never claimed to be a *faylasūf*, however "philosophic" some of his works may be in a modern sense.

146 18.8-10. "this class of persons . . . without a teacher": See 5.21, and note 48 on the requisites of philosophic understanding. Since the persons referred to here are *ex hypothesi* men of natural intellectual ability, they can only be misled through lack of one of the other requisites: sound morals (i.e. "practical virtue") or sound intellectual education.

147 18.14. " 'Associating . . . wrong' ": *Qur'ān*, xxxi, 12, illustrating the proportionate relation between the value of the being and the greatness of the injury.

148 18.16-17. "If it were not . . . on the subject": Cf. *Tahāfut*, pp. 209-10, 358, 588, Ibn Ṭufayl, *Ḥayy*, p. ١٠٠, for similar assertions.

[CHAPTER THREE]

149 18.21. "especially of noble beings": Cf. Aristotle, *Eth. Nic.*, vi, 7, 1141a9-b3: Wisdom (*sophia*) is intuition and scientific knowledge of the most noble things by nature. There are beings much more divine than man, such as the heavenly bodies.

150 18.20-19.1. "True science . . . misery in the next life": Cf. *Summary of Aristotle, Metaph.*, pp. 2-3: classification of the sciences as theoretical, practical and logical, following Aristotle; see S. Van den Bergh, *Epitome*, n. 21 for references.

"in the next life": *ukhrāwīya, ukhrāwī*. Happiness and misery in a future life imply individual survival, and Ibn Rushd did not believe in this. But the statement is unmistakable, if not here and in 14.20, then certainly in 22.7; and explicitly in *Manāhij*, 122.6, "states of happiness or misery after death". These are two exoteric books, and Ibn Rushd's true opinions must be sought in his commentaries on Aristotle's *De animā.*

151 19.1-2. "the acts which bring happiness . . . misery": In *Comm. on Pl. Rep.*, I, xi, 5-7, Ibn Rushd endorses Plato's view that happiness is not a reward and misery not a punishment; both are *effects* of the corresponding acts.

152 19.7. "the other sort": *al-jins ath-thānī*, lit. "the second sort". Evidently Ibn Rushd has mentally reversed the order.

153 19.7-9. "as people . . . '*The revival of the sciences of religion*' ": I.e. he called it by the name of the whole because it dealt with the

most important part. *Iḥyā' 'ulūm ad-dīn*, written by Ghazālī in the years following his departure from Baghdād in 1095.

[154] 19.10. "teaching is of two classes, [of] concepts and [of] judgements": *kān at-ta'līm ṣinfayn taṣawwuran wa taṣdīqan*, lit. "teaching was two classes, concept (or conception) and judgement". Ibn Rushd's exposition of these two logical concepts is excessively concise, and his use of each of them is not free from ambiguity. The classical accounts in Arabic are Fārābī, *'Uyūn al-masā'il*, in Dieterici, XIV, p. 56, and Ghazālī, *Maqāṣid al-falāsifa* (Cairo, 1936), pp. 4-5. The origin of the doctrine is perhaps to be found in Sextus Empiricus, *Adversus logicos*, viii (ii), 11-12. For further explanation and comments, see the following notes; H. A. Wolfson, "The terms *taṣawwur* and *taṣdīq* in Arabic philosophy and their Greek, Latin and Hebrew equivalents", *Moslem World*, 33 (1943), pp. 114-28; and "The double faith theory", *Jewish Quarterly Review*, N.S. 33 (1942-43), pp. 213-64.

[155] 19.11. "the logicians": *ahl al-'ilm bil-kalām*. The phrase is ambiguous, since *kalām* may be taken either in its primary sense of "rational discourse", Gk. *logos*, or in its specialized Islamic sense of "reasoned theology". Evidently in this context Ibn Rushd does not refer to the *mutakallimūn*, who had not contributed to developing these doctrines; but he does not wish to use the philosophical name for logic, *manṭiq*.

[156] 19.11-12. "the methods . . . rhetorical": In the Greco-Arabic logic *taṣdīq*, "judgement", is the act of affirming a proposition as true or denying it as false, i.e. of assent to it or dissent from it. Judgements are classified as primary (*awwalī*), i.e. known immediately like mathematical axioms or facts of sensation; or acquired (*muktasab*), learned through reasoning from previously known judgements. (Ghazālī, *Maqāṣid*, pp. 4-5). I think Ibn Rushd is here speaking of the second kind only, judgements reached by reasoning, since all three methods are kinds of argument. Wolfson's classification of judgements arrived at by the rhetorical method as "primary" in this passage is not borne out by the following passage, 19.17-20.14, where the rhetorical method is spoken of in terms of syllogisms with premisses and conclusions. H. A. Wolfson in *Moslem World*, 33 (1943), and *Jewish Quarterly Review*, N.S. 33 (1942-43).

Taṣdīq in this passage is sometimes regarded from the learner's or receptive viewpoint, sometimes from the teacher's or expressive viewpoint; it has therefore to be translated as "arriving at judgements" or "bringing about assent" according to the context. (In the same way the three methods are sometimes spoken of as methods of assent by the believers and sometimes as methods of summons by Scripture.) It also sometimes refers to the act itself, "judgement".

[157] 19.12-13. "two methods . . . a symbol of it": *taṣawwur* is apprehension of concepts, representation in the passive intellect of the form (*ṣūra*) or idea (*ma'nā*) of a certain kind of thing. Ghazālī, *Maqāṣid*, p. 4: "Every judgement is necessarily preceded by two conceptions, for he who does not understand 'the world' alone and 'created' alone cannot conceivably judge that it [the world] is created." Here too there is a distinction of primary concepts (simple, such as "being", "thing") and acquired (complex, such as "body", "sun", "intellect"). But this bears no correspondence to the distinction of two methods of conception here. Ibn Rushd is thinking of the contrast between direct representation of a thing itself and representation of a symbol of it (*mithāluhu*), which stands for it. Being imaginative, a symbol is often more readily understood by ordinary minds than a concept which may be highly abstract. Cf. Fārābī, *Siyāsāt*, p. 55; *Taḥṣīl*, pp. 40-41. The "symbol" referred to here is not language as symbolic of concepts; it is one concept symbolic of another, as in allegory.

[158] 19.21-20.1. "the prevailing methods . . . judgements": On the two "common methods" (*aṭ-ṭuruq al-mushtaraka*), the dialectical and rhetorical, cf. 15.12 and note 126. On the aims of Scripture, cf. *Tahāfut*, pp. 582-83.

[159] 20.1-2. "of four classes": Ibn Rushd in the following section classifies the common methods on a new basis, applying it to dialectical and rhetorical arguments alike. Dividing the syllogism into two parts, premisses and conclusion, he considers whether each part is really symbolic of some other judgement or judgements, i.e. is an allegorical statement, or expresses its real meaning directly. Four combinations are then possible:

1. Direct premisses + direct conclusion
2. Direct premisses + symbolic conclusion
3. Symbolic premisses + direct conclusion
4. Symbolic premisses + symbolic conclusion

Now whenever a statement (premiss or conclusion) in Scripture ought to be understood in its direct meaning by all classes of people, it has the same meaning for the dialectical and rhetorical class as for the demonstrative class, and is thus "certain", true or correct, for the former as for the latter. But this result is "accidental" because to the two lower classes the statement is not known by demonstrative methods but "based on accepted ideas" (*mashhūra*) or "based on opinions" (*maẓnūna*). On the other hand a statement in Scripture which is really symbolic is usually not understood as such by the lower classes, but taken in its direct sense; and this is not even accidentally certain, since it is not the true meaning of the statement.

How symbolic and direct statements can be combined in the same arguments is obscure, in the absence of examples.

160 20.2. "specialized": *khāṣṣa*, i.e. related to the élite, *al-khawāṣṣ*, the demonstrative class; the relation is explained in what follows.

161 20.4. "based on accepted ideas or on opinions": *mashhūra aw maẓnūna*. Premisses that are *mashhūra* are dialectical; premisses that are *maẓnūna*, known by *ẓann*, are rhetorical. See note 25.

162 20.20. "popular": *jumhūrīya*. We should expect "dialectical" *jadalīya*, since Ibn Rushd is speaking of the superior common method, and below, 21.2-3, he says that the masses (*al-jumhūr*) should not know such interpretations. It seems that Ibn Rushd is using *jumhūrīya* here in a broad sense, to embrace both the lower classes.

163 20.20-21.1. "Such interpretations . . . statements": See note 69.

164 21.5-6. "no man of sound intellect is exempted from this kind of assent": I.e. no sane person falls below the qualifications which oblige him to have at least this kind of assent. But some, namely the other two classes, go beyond it.

165 21.8. "training": *aṣ-ṣinā'a*, lit. "art", then any acquired skill or science.

166 21.11-12. "The reason for that [in the case of the latter]": *as-sabab fī dhālika*. The reason given here applies only to the hearer. The reason why the explainer is an unbeliever is given in the next section, 21.21 ff.

167 21.16-18. "They should not be expressed . . . ambiguous": The text is uncertain. See Hourani, *ad loc.*, and N. Golb in Heb. n. 441. On the best interpretation the thought is obscurely formulated. I think the situation mentioned here is probably the same as that which I have numbered [2, i] in *Manāhij*, pp. 124-27. See esp. 126.7-8: "when it is difficult to understand the context in both respects, i.e. that it is a symbol and what it symbolizes, but there arises at first glance a suspicion of the imagination that it is symbolic". At any rate the treatment is the same in both cases.

168 21.19. " 'And no one . . . except God' ": *Qur'ān*, iii, 7. See notes 87 and 138.

169 21.20-21. " 'And they will ask you . . . a little knowledge' ": *Qur'ān*, xvii, 85. "The Spirit" is traditionally interpreted as the angel Gabriel. Cf. *Qur'ān*, xvi, 102.

170 21.21-22.1. "As for the man . . . unbelief": Cf. *Tahāfut*, p. 362: "the man who has proved its evidence is forbidden to reveal it to the man who has no power to discover its truth, for he would be like his murderer."

[171] 22.2. "the Legislator": *ash-shāriʿ*, i.e. the Prophet Muhammad. Cf. *Manāhij*, 27.16.

[172] 22.3. "a group of people of our time": I have found no clue to their identity. That they claimed to be philosophers is evident from the next sentence and from 26.2. This means that Ibn Rushd is not here speaking of the *mutakallimūn*, who disclaimed any relation to *falsafa*. Yet he goes back to speaking of the *mutakallimūn* in the next section, 23.18 ff. 26.1 ff. shows that he blames two different groups, some pseudo-philosophers and the *mutakallimūn*. See note 195.

[173] 22.7. "in this world and the next": *fid-dunyā wal-ākhira*. Cf. 18.20-19.1 and note 150.

[174] 22.7. "a parable": *mithāl*, the same word as that used for "symbol". Ibn Rushd's parable of the doctor and his detractors is of evident Platonic inspiration: see W. Jaeger, *Paideia* (Oxford, 1939-45), II and III, *passim*, on the importance of the parallel of medicine and philosophy in Plato's thought. But I have not located the parable itself in Plato's dialogues. Perhaps the closest parallel in Plato is his parable of the shipmaster and his crew in *Republic*, vi, 488a-489c. Cf. *Manāhij*, pp. 68 ff.

[175] 22.19. "if he . . . true allegories . . .": One of the lessons of the parable is that even true allegories should not be taught to the majority. The implication is that the Legislator intended to treat them with statements ("apparent" meanings) which are in themselves strictly false. Cf. esp. *Comm. on Pl. Rep.*, I, xii, 6: "Just as it is only the doctor who administers the drug, so it is the king in the exercise of rulership who employs a lie towards the masses. For lying tales are necessary for the education of the citizens. There is no lawgiver who does not employ fictitious tales, because this is necessary for the masses if they are to obtain happiness." See my introd., pp. 33-34, 37-38.

[176] 22.21-23.1. "this will lead them to think . . . cure disease": Cf. *Comm. on Pl. Rep.*, II, iii, 6: The sick do not consider medicine to be the art of healing or that the restoration of health is possible, so they do not respect or trust doctors; they throw stones at them.

[177] 23.3. "certain": *yaqīnīyan*. L. Gauthier, *Théorie*, p. 81, n. 1, and Gr., n. 63, points out that *yaqīnī* is equivalent to "demonstrative" and that the implication is that one can reason from one case to the other.

[178] 23.4-7. "It presents a true analogy . . . the health of souls"; Cf. Pl. *Rep.*, iii, 409c ff., doctors and judges; 444, virtue the health of the soul. See W. Jaeger, *Paideia*, II and III.

[179] 23.9-10. " 'Fasting . . . fear God' ": *Qur'ān*, ii, 183.

[180] 23.10-11. " 'Their flesh . . . touch him' ": *Qur'ān*, xxii, 37.

[181] 23.11. " 'Prayer . . . transgression' ": *Qur'ān*, xxix, 45.

[182] 23.17-18. " 'We offered . . .' the verse": *Qur'ān*, xxxiii, 72. The verse continues: 'But they refused to hold it and shied away from it, and man held it.' There is obscurity in *amāna*, "deposit": to what does it refer? Ibn Rushd's interpretation is far-fetched.

[183] 23.20-24.1. "Thus the Mu'tazilites . . . less frequently": See note 69.

[184] 24.1-2. "In consequence . . . divided people": Cf. *Manāhij*, pp. 69-70: The *mutakallimūn*, who are dialecticians, have been the cause of the growth of sects in Islam.

[185] 24.3-4. "their methods were ⟨more⟩ obscure . . . demonstration": *Manāhij* contains many illustrations of these weaknesses, e.g. on pp. 29 ff., 40-41, 48-51, 52-53, 73. Ghazālī makes similar criticisms. *Qisṭās*, p. 201: the *mutakallimūn* neglect the details of accurate reasoning.

[186] 24.5-6. "many of the principles . . . sophistical": Cf. *Summary of Aristotle, Metaph.*, pp. 171-72: The Ash'arite views on ethics (theistic subjectivism) are "like those of Protagoras". *Comm. on Pl. Rep.*, I, xi, 3: Ash'arite ethics is sophistical.

[187] 24.6-8. "they deny . . . secondary causes": Cf. Ben Maymōn, *Guide*, 1, chs. 71-76, a slashing criticism of the Ash'arites, also from an Aristotelian point of view.

[188] 24.18-19. "the three methods . . . the special method": See Hourani, note C, on the difficulties of interpretation of these words. By inserting "namely", *hādhihi hiya*, we get a statement which agrees perfectly with Ibn Rushd's usual doctrine of the three methods.

"the special method": *al-khāṣṣa*. It is grammatically possible to understand *al-khāṣṣa* as "the élite", following "instruction of", *ta'līm*; this is how the Hebrew translator understood it. But this interpretation fails to provide a third method.

[189] 25.6-9. "So whoever wishes . . . to everyone": This sentence provides the programme for *Manāhij*. This is clear from 25.19-20, "It is our desire to devote our time to this object"; and *Manāhij*, 27.15 ff., "In this book I think fit to inquire into the apparent meaning of the dogmas", following the intention of the Legislator. *Manāhij*, p. 27, also contains a backward reference to *Faṣl* and its contents. But in fact *Manāhij* is more like a handbook for teachers, and contains much polemic against the sects and particularly the Ash'arites. (See my introd., pp. 36-37.) The last pages of *Manāhij*, 124-27, go into more detail on the correct policy in revealing and concealing allegorical interpretation; and finally, p. 127, Ibn Rushd announces an intention to apply the policy in more detail to the individual passages of Scripture. But this last programme was not fulfilled in any subsequent book. For the rest of his working life Ibn Rushd was fully occupied by the commentaries on Aristotle, the *Tahāfut* and his public duties.

The intended programme of *Manāhij* may be compared with Ghazālī's handbook of popular dogmatics, *K. al-iqtiṣād fīl-i'tiqād.*

Ibn Rushd's programme amounts to Zahirism (for the people) in doctrine, i.e. imposition of the literal meaning of Scripture and prohibition of popular theology (*kalām*). This is parallel to the Zahirite policy of Ibn Tūmart and the first three Almohad monarchs in law: they compiled for popular use collections of Traditions on purification, booty, wine, prayer and *jihād*: Marrākushi, *Mu'jib*, pp. 183, 202-3; I. Goldziher, *Z.D.M.G.*, 41 (1887), pp. 81-99, and Introd. to *Ibn Toumert*, pp. 43-51. Eventually Abū Yūsuf (1184-1198/9) suppressed the science of applied law (*'ilm al-furū'*) of the Malikite rite: Marrākushī, *Mu'jib*, pp. 201-3.

190 25.10. "mastering their meaning": *nuṣratihā.* The word is puzzling, here and in 25.15. *Nuṣra* normally means "aid, assistance, victory, conquest", like *naṣr*: see Lane. In *Manāhij*, 77.6, *al-qā'imīn bi-nuṣratihi*, "undertake its defence"; also Fārābī, *Iḥṣā'*, pp. 107-8, "defence". But this is inappropriate here. Fārābī, *Iḥṣā'*, p. 64, has *ḥafẓihi aw nuṣratihi*, which seems to mean "its retention or acquisition"; and "acquisition" is more appropriate. Gr. translates "force de persuasion"; followed by Alonso. Heb. has *mashmīrethem*, "observing them". I have rendered it in a way that suits the context and is not too far from the meaning "victory, conquest".

191 25.9-12. "For if the sayings . . . not apparent in them": This deliberately enigmatic quality is attributed by Fārābī to the writings of Plato and Aristotle. *Compendium legum*, ed. F. Gabrieli in *Plato Arabus*, III (London, 1952), p. 4: "The wise Plato did not allow himself to reveal the sciences and uncover them to all the people; so he followed the method of symbols (*ar-ramz*) and enigmas (*al-alghāz*), causing blindness and difficulty, lest science should fall into the hands of unsuitable people and be wasted", etc. *Risāla fī mā yanbaghī*, in Dieterici, XIV, pp. 53-54: purposeful obscurity in Aristotle. *Jam'*, pp. 5-7: Plato and Aristotle. Ibn Sīnā, *Najāt*, pp. 499-500: the duty of the prophet is to conceal difficult matters from the public, while using enigmas and hints (*rumūz wa ishārāt*) to summon those qualified to philosophic research. Ben Maymōn, *Guide*, Introduction, Eng. tr. M. Friedländer, 2nd ed., pp. 4 ff.: The Bible often speaks figuratively "in order that the uneducated may comprehend it according to the measure of their faculties and the feebleness of their apprehension, while educated persons may take it in a different sense". Following Proverbs, xxv, 11, he likens wise language to a golden apple overlaid with a filigree network of silver; only the keen-sighted observe the gold underneath the silver (p. 6).

See note 142.

192 25.14. "their miraculous character": *al-i'jāz*. So Ibn Rushd believed in at least one miracle! And the fact is confirmed by *Manāhij*, pp. 100-3, and *Tahāfut*, p. 515. It is true that these are all exoteric works, but they do show that their author was willing to confess the *Qur'ān* a miracle and give this fact a prominent place in his system of popular religion. Does this prove that Ibn Rushd was not a rationalist? Alonso says "Yes", Gauthier says "No", and by the time they have defined "rationalist" we conclude that both are probably right and "the disagreement . . . is . . . almost resolvable into a disagreement about naming" (11.16-17). All that really matters is to determine what Ibn Rushd thought. The question is too large for an exhaustive treatment here, but I shall draw the implications of the three passages referred to above.

The present passage in *Faṣl* merely indicates that the *Qur'ān* has *unique* qualities not found in any other book. Nothing is said about how these qualities were produced in it, so that "miraculous" may quite well mean only "natural but extraordinary".

In *Manāhij*, the most fundamental proof that the *Qur'ān* is "preternatural and miraculous" (*khāriq wa mu'jiz*) is that "the Laws of doctrine and practice contained in it are not of a sort that could possibly be discovered by a learning process, but only by inspiration (*bi-waḥy*)" (100.8-9). This passage and that which follows seem to express a theory of miracle in the full sense of *khāriq al-'āda*, that which interrupts the ordinary course of nature. But we must remember that *Manāhij* is an account of what the masses should believe, and does not therefore raise the pertinent deeper questions, such as: What is meant by *khāriq*, *mu'jiz* and *waḥy*?

The passage in *Tahāfut*, p. 515, is somewhat ambiguous. First Ibn Rushd says that the prophet can interrupt the ordinary course of nature, within the limits of what is logically possible. Then he comes to the *Qur'ān* and writes: "The clearest of miracles is the Venerable Book of Allah, the existence of which is not an interruption of the course of nature assumed by tradition, like the changing of a rod into a serpent, but its miraculous nature is established by way of perception and consideration for every man who has been or who will be till the day of resurrection" (515.11-15, Eng. tr. S. Van den Bergh). Here, as Van den Bergh says in his note 315.4, "he does not admit that prophets can interrupt the course of nature, but is unwilling to express it too clearly".

A final answer to the question of Ibn Rushd's theory of the miracle of the *Qur'ān* would have to be based on a full consideration of his views on causality and on inspiration. My present impression is that such a firm Aristotelian could not possibly have accepted any *khāriq al-'āda* in the Ash'arite sense, an event willed by God in defiance of natural laws of cause and effect.

[193] 25.16-17. "(3) They contain means ... allegorical meaning"; One of the "means of drawing attention" (*tanbīh*) has been explained in 8.11-12: the apparent contradictions in Scripture, which stimulate the observant to seek a deeper understanding of it.

[194] 25.19-20. "It is our desire ... effectively": I.e. the programme mentioned in 25.6-9. See note 189.

[195] 26.2. "who claim an affinity with philosophy": L. Gauthier, "Scolastique musulmane et scolastique chrétienne", p. 247, takes this as an obvious reference to Ibn Sīnā, on the ground of Ibn Rushd's normal attitude to Ibn Sīnā. But it seems more natural to connect the phrase with 22.3-4, "a group of people of our time ... some of them thinking that they were being philosophic"; and Ibn Sīnā was by no means a contemporary, *min ahl zamāninā*, having died 140 years before *Faṣl*. Cf. Ibn Ṭufayl, *Ḥayy*, p. ١٥٥: we have been induced to reveal hidden science by "the false opinions appearing in our time, put out and expressed publicly by the pseudo-philosophers of the age", *mutafalsifat al-ʿaṣr*.

[196] 26.10. "this triumphant rule": *hādh al-amr al-ghālib*. I have translated the phrase somewhat ambiguously, in order to reflect the ambiguity of the Arabic.

(1) *amr* may be "rule" in the sense of "régime": the phrase then refers to the victorious dynasty of the Almohades and gives them credit for removing strife among sects. It is taken thus by I. Goldziher, Introd. to *Ibn Toumert*, p. 81, and by L. Gauthier, *Théorie*, p. 89, and *Traité*, tr. and n. 77; it is also my preference. Alonso, p. 199, n. 2, finds a great difficulty in the implication of this version, that the ruler was opposed to the Ashʿarite doctrine of Ibn Tūmart, the Mahdī and founder of the dynasty. The passage, however, stresses a positive method, "summoning the masses to a middle way" (26.12), etc., and does not imply an active suppression of the Ashʿarites. In any case it is very probable that Abū Yaʿqūb had abandoned Ashʿarite opinions, in view of his interest in philosophy.

(2) *amr* may be "matter", and the phrase may be understood as "this prevalent method": thus Alonso, "principalmente con el metodo que yo indico". But *amr* is now vague, and in what way is Ibn Rushd's method "prevalent", *ghālib*? The following passage indicates a measure which has had some public impact.

The "benefits" to the class of scientists and philosophers can well refer to the dynasty's protection and encouragement of them, and the "middle way" for the masses may be their learning of the collections of Traditions made by the dynasty. Marrākushī says that Abū Yaʿqūb collected the Traditions on *jihād* and dictated them to his army, *c.* A.D. 1179: *Muʿjib*, p. 183.

[197] 26.13. "the followers of authority": *al-muqallidīn*, those '*ulamā*' who derived their opinions and decisions on points of applied

law from the works of the four great lawyers (in this case the *Muwaṭṭā* of Mālik Ibn Anas) and not directly from the Scriptures.

[APPENDIX: *Ḍamīma*]

198 "[*Ḍamīma*]": This title, meaning "Appendix", has no manuscript authority, but was applied to this little essay by Müller and has been retained by subsequent editors. It is essentially fitting to consider this work as an appendix to *Faṣl*, since it expands an answer given there, and is referred to there at 11.6, in the words "We have devoted a separate essay (*qawl*) to this question, impelled by one of our friends"; the title given in the Escurial manuscript, "The question mentioned", etc., refers back to this sentence. On the use of the past tense "We have devoted", *afradnā*, see Gr., Introd. to *Traité*, p. vi: it does not imply that the essay was published or even written before *Faṣl*.

But the essay is in no sense an appendix to *Manāhij*, and should not have been printed after it by Müller and Alonso.

199 128.3. "May God . . . misfortunes": Gr., n. 80, shows, on the whole convincingly, that the anonymous person to whom the essay is addressed is probably the Almohad monarch himself, Abū Ya'qūb. The terms of address, especially the reference to "your power", *'izzatakum*, and the use of the plural of majesty, are uniquely fitting to a ruler. We know from Marrākushī, *Mu'jib*, pp. 174-75, that Abū Ya'qūb was highly interested in philosophy, and Ibn Rushd there gives an opinion of him that closely parallels his remark here in 128.4: "I perceived in him such a copious memory as I did not think could be found even in any one of those who concerned themselves full time with this subject" (p. 175). Cf. also *Comm. on Pl. Rep.*, III, xxi, 1, and Rosenthal's note.

There remains a doubt whether the philosopher could have referred to the king as "one of our friends", *ba'ḍ aṣḥābinā*, in *Faṣl*, 11.6. It is one thing to address a king as "brother", *yā akhī*, in private conversation, as Ibn Rushd addressed Abū Yusūf (Ibn Abī Uṣaybi'a, *'Uyūn al-anbā'*, p. 74), but quite a different matter to refer to him as "a friend" in a published work. And if he did so at the monarch's own request, in order not to publicize his interest in philosophy, then why does Ibn Rushd hint at that interest so broadly at the beginning of *Ḍamīma*? I leave these questions unanswered, but incline to think that in spite of them the "friend" probably was Abū Ya'qūb. This opinion is confirmed by the notable care and lucidity with which the problem is treated.

200 128.5. "the difficulty . . . Knowledge": See note 93 for references to other passages in which Ibn Rushd treats the problem.

[201] 128.7-8. "for he . . . untie it": The saying is derived from Aristotle, *Metaphysics*, B, 1, 995a 27-30. Used again by Ibn Rushd in *Tafsīr*, pp. 167-68.

[202] 128.13-14. "but that . . . eternal knowledge": The doctrine of God's unchangeability goes back at least to Plato; see esp. *Republic*, ii, 379-82, a perfect God cannot change either for better or for worse.

[203] 128.17. "the existent and the non-existent": *al-mawjūd wal-ma'dūm*. In the whole discussion Ibn Rushd avoids the technical terms "actual", *bil-fi'l*, and "potential", *bil-quwwa*.

[204] 129.15-16. "as we have explained it to you in conversation": Gr., n. 80, thinks it "fort possible" that the occasion was the same as that of the original interview, *c.* 1168, when the question of the eternity of the world was discussed and would lead easily to a discussion about God's creative Knowledge. Certainly this is possible; but it is likely that Ibn Rushd talked philosophy with Abū Ya'qūb on many later occasions, and we have no means of deciding when or how often this particular topic was discussed. The last time was probably not long before *Ḍamīma*, because of certain phrases in the opening paragraph: *intahā* (128.4); "ending your perplexity" (128, 5-6)—one would not leave one's king in perplexity for years.

[205] 129.17-18. "Abū Ḥāmid . . . no conviction": *Tahāfut al-falāsifa*, 13th discussion, pp. 229-31; quoted in *Tahāfut at-tahāfut*, p. 459.

[206] 130.2. "Zayd": Gr. emends to "the column", and follows with a series of emendations to correspond. See his notes 83-84. My reasons for retaining the original text of the Escurial MS. are explained in Hourani, note D.

[207] 131.5. "purification [of concepts]": *at-tanzīh*, i.e. clearing our concepts of God's nature of human attributes. Ibn Rushd claims that his *tanzīh* goes further than that of contemporary theologians, who imagine that both divine and human knowledge can be embraced by a single definition (*Faṣl*, 11.5). But it admits that God has some kind of knowledge of particulars (131.1-3). Cf. *Tafsīr*, pp. 1705-8: God's Knowledge is not to be described as either universal or particular (though in His own way He knows both universals and particulars). *Tanzīh* of other aspects of God is dealt with in *Manāhij*, pp. 58-78.

[208] 131.8-9. "'Does He not know . . . the Omniscient!'": *Qur'ān*, lxvii, 14.

[209] 131.10. "unqualified": as universal or particular. Cf. *Tafsīr*, pp. 1705-8; *Faṣl*, 11.13.

[210] 131.11-13. "And how is it conceivable . . . inspiration?": Cf. *Faṣl*, 11.6-10 and note 98.

[EXTRACT: *Manāhij*, pp. 122-27]

211 "[THE FUTURE LIFE]": The following chapter deals with the last of five topics of doctrine, from the point of view of *Manāhij*: What should be taught to the people as the doctrine of the *Qur'ān?*

212 122.5. Summary: For the doctrine of this section, the superiority of corporeal symbols for the masses, cf. *Tahāfut*, p. 585. Aristotle, *Metaphysics*, α, 3, 995a 4-6: "The force of habit is shown by the laws, in which the legendary and childish elements prevail over our knowledge about them, owing to habit"; and Ibn Rushd's comments, *Tafsīr*, pp. 42-43: The laws have been laid down for imparting virtue to the people, not for acquainting them with the truth, so it has fashioned parables for them. Cf. *Faṣl*, 15.8-16, and note 126; 16.5-10.

213 122.6-7. "states of happiness or misery after death": Cf. *Faṣl*, 18.20-19.1 and note 150.

214 122.17-20. "One [sub-] group . . . enumerating them": This is the philosophic position that drew Ghazālī's criticism in *Fayṣal*, p. 91, that the philosophers make the corporeal symbolization a matter of expediency only. It should also be the position of Ibn Rushd: in the Greek philosophic tradition a body in the next life is not only useless but an encumbrance, hindering the realization of the soul's ends. But Ibn Rushd is not frank on the future life in his public writings: cf. note 139. Here he even seems to divert attention from his own view by passing over it rapidly and considering at greater length another learned position. See Alonso, p. 347, n. 1.

215 123.1-3. "Ibn 'Abbās . . . 'except the names' ": Specifically, there are things in both worlds called "bodies", but they differ totally in their natures. For another case of homonymy, *ishtirāk al-ism*, cf. *Faṣl*, 11.2-4, the two kinds of "knowledge". The same quotation is used in a similar context in *Tahāfut*, p. 585. Tradition not located in Wensinck, *Concordance*.

216 123.3. "more suitable for the élite": Cf. *Tahāfut*, p. 586: "it must be assumed that what arises from the dead is simulacra of these earthly bodies, not these bodies themselves". See S. Van den Bergh's note, 362.1. Both these passages lend apparent support to the opinion of M. Horten in *Texte zu dem Streite*, that this was Ibn Rushd's real view. But see note 214. It should be observed that in both passages the argument is directed against (1) the return of our earthly bodies, not against (2a) the absence of bodies.

217 123.5. "the return of the soul to other bodies": Why is "soul" singular, with "bodies" plural? Is there an allusion to the unity of soul?

218 123.12. "this state of affairs": i.e. simultaneous existence of bodies composed of the same material.

[219] 123.12-16. "The truth . . . their intellects": Cf. *Faṣl*, pp. 14-15, 17; *Tahāfut*, pp. 582, 585-86; Ghazālī, *Fayṣal*, pp. 90-92.

[220] 123.16. Summary. The argument of the following section is stated more simply in *Tahāfut*, p. 557: "And the comparison of death with sleep in this question is an evident proof that the soul survives, since the activity of the soul ceases in sleep through the inactivity of its organ, but the existence of the soul does not cease, and therefore it is necessary that its condition in death should be like its condition in sleep, for the parts follow the same rule" (Eng. tr. S. Van den Bergh). See S. Van den Bergh, note 343.7.

[221] 123.18-19. " 'God receives . . .' the verse": *Qur'ān*, xxxix, 42. The rest of the verse: 'He keeps those for whom He has decreed death, and lets the others go until a stated time. Truly in that there are signs for a people who reflect.'

[222] 124.5-6. "As the Philosopher . . . 'sees' ": Aristotle, *De animā*, i, 4, 408b 21. I.e. the condition of the organ makes all the difference to the function, while the substance (soul) remains unchanged.

[223] 124.7. Summary: The following section works out more elaborately the policy stated in *Faṣl*, pp. 20-21 and elsewhere: that allegorical interpretations should not be revealed to the masses more than can be avoided.

[224] 124.12-13. "the idea really intended": *al-ma'nā al-mawjūd fī nafsihi*, lit. "the idea which exists in itself".

[225] 124.14. "symbolization": See notes 62 and 157 on the kind of symbolization Ibn Rushd has in mind.

[226] 124.21-125.1. "The fourth . . . symbol": An example of this sub-class would have been helpful, but none is given, here or below, p. 126.

[227] 125.7. "towards it": *ilayhi*, i.e. towards allegorical interpretation.

[228] 125.8. " 'The Black Stone . . . on earth' ": Cf. Ghazālī, *Fayṣal*, p. 86: This was one of three Traditions that even Ibn Ḥanbal had to interpret allegorically.

[229] 125.14. "*the distinction*": *Fayṣal*, pp. 80-85. See *Faṣl*, 15.15-16 and note 127.

[230] 125.17. "more persuasive": Considerations of persuasiveness are explicitly rejected by Ghazālī: see *Fayṣal*, in *Jawāhir*, pp. 90-91; *Tahāfut al-falāsifa*, ed. M. Bouyges (Beirut, 1927), pp. 355-56—20th question. But his own theory of religious instruction seems to involve such considerations; see above, Introduction, pp. 33-34, and note 142 to the translation.

[231] 125.20-21. " 'There is nothing . . . the Fire' ": See Wensinck, *Concordance*, s.v. *ra'a*. Bukhārī, iii, 24, etc.

[232] 125.21-126.1. " 'Between . . . basin' ": Wensinck, *Concordance*, s.v. *ḥawd*; Bukhārī, xx, 5, etc.

[233] 126.1-2. " 'Dust . . . *os coccygis*' ": Muslim, *Fitn*, 142. Murray's *New English dictionary*, s.v. *Coccyx*: "The small triangular bone appended to the point of the sacrum and forming the termination of the spinal column in man."

[234] 126.9. "idle": *bāṭila*. In this context it must mean "useless" or "harmful", not "false", because here it is not false that there is symbolism.

[235] 127.4-7. "It is our desire . . . these four classes": See note 189 on this programme.

[236] 127.10. "575": i.e. A.D. 1179/80.

LIST OF ABBREVIATIONS AND EDITIONS USED

Allard, M., "Le rationalisme d'Averroès": "Le rationalisme d'Averroès d'après une étude sur la création", *Bulletin d'Études Orientales,* 14 (1952-54), pp. 7-59. (Institut français de Damas, Damascus, 1954.)

Alonso: Alonso, M., *Teología de Averroes* (Madrid-Granada, 1947).

Ar.: Arabic.

Aristotle, *Anal. post.*: *Analytica posteriora.*

Eth. Nic.: *Ethica Nicomachea.*

Metaph.: *Metaphysica.*

Soph. elench.: *Sophistici elenchi.*

Asín Palacios, M., *Abenházam: Abenházam de Córdoba y su historia critica de las ideas religiosas* (Madrid, 1928-31), 4 vols.

Ibn Masarra: Ibn Masarra y su escuela, 2nd ed. in his *Obras escogidas,* I (Madrid, 1946).

Justo medio: El justo medio en la creencia; compendio de teología dogmatica (Madrid, 1929).

Ben Maymōn, *Guide*: *The guide for the perplexed,* Eng. tr. M. Friedländer, 2nd ed. (London, 1904).

Dieterici: Dieterici, F., *Die Philosophie der Araber* (Leiden, 1890).

Fārābī, *De Platonis philosophia,* ed. F. Rosenthal and R. Walzer in *Plato Arabus,* III (London, 1943).

Iḥṣā'al-'ulūm, 2nd ed. U. M. Amīn (Cairo, 1948).

Jam': Kitāb al-jam' bayna ra'yay al-ḥakīmayn Aflāṭūn al-ilāhī wa Arisṭūṭālīs, in Dieterici, XIV.

Comm. on Risālat Zaynūn: Sharḥ risālat Zaynūn al-kabīr al-Yūnānī, in *Rasā'il al-Fārābī* (Hyderabad, 1926).

Risāla fī mā yanbaghī: Risāla . . . fī mā yanbaghī an yuqaddam qabla ta'allum al-falsafa, in Dieterici, XIV.

Siyāsāt: Kitāb as-siyāsāt al-madanīya, in *Rasā'il al-Fārābī* (Hyderabad, 1926).

Taḥṣīl as-sa'āda, in *Rasā'il al-Fārābī* (Hyderabad, 1926).

Gauthier, L., *Ibn Rochd: Ibn Rochd (Averroès)* (Paris, 1948).

"Scolastique musulmane et scolastique chrétienne", *Revue d'histoire de la philosophie,* 2 (1928), pp. 221-53, 333-65.

Traité: See Gr.

Théorie: La théorie d'Ibn Rochd (Averroès) sur les rapports de la religion et de la philosophie (Paris, 1909).

Ghazālī, *Fayṣal: Kitāb fayṣal at-tafriqa bayn al-Islām waz-zandaqa*, in *Jawāhir*.

Iḥyā': *Iḥyā' 'ulūm ad-dīn*, 'Irāqī ed. (Cairo, 1938-39).

Iljām: *Kitāb iljām al-'awāmm 'an 'ilm al-kalām* (Cairo, 1933; Munīrīya Press). Span. tr. in *Justo medio*.

Mīzān al-'amal, ed. Kurdī (Cairo, 1910). Fr. tr. H. Hāshim, *Le critère de l'action* (Paris, 1945).

Munqidh: *Kitāb al-munqidh min aḍ-ḍalāl*, ed. J. Ṣalībā and K. 'Ayyād (Damascus, 1939).

Qisṭās: *Kitāb al-qisṭās al-mustaqīm*, in *Jawāhir*.

Tahāfut al-falāsifa, ed. M. Bouyges (Beirut, 1927).

Gk.: Greek.

Goichon: Goichon, A.-M., *Lexique de la langue philosophique d'Ibn Sīnā* (Paris, 1938).

Goldhizer, I., Introd. to *Ibn Toumert*: *Le livre de Mohammed Ibn Toumert, mahdi des Almohades*, ed. J. D. Luciani (Algiers, 1903).

Zâhiriten: *Die Zâhiriten, ihr Lehrsystem und ihre Geschichte* (Leipzig, 1884).

Z.D.M.G., 41 (1887): "Materielien zur Kenntniss der Almohadenbewegung", *Zeitschrift der Deutschen Morgenländischen Gesellschaft*, 41 (1887), pp. 30-140.

Gr.: Gauthier, L., *Ibn Rochd (Averroès)*: *Traité décisif (façl el-maqâl) sur l'accord de la religion et de la philosophie*, Ar. and Fr. tr., 3rd ed. (Algiers, 1948).

Heb.: "The Hebrew translation of Averroes' *Faṣl al-maqāl*", ed. N. Golb, *Proceedings of the American Academy for Jewish Research*, 25 (1956), pp. 91-113, and 26 (1957), pp. 41-64.

Homenaje: *Homenaje á D. Francisco Codera* (Saragossa, 1904).

Horten, M., *Texte zu dem Streite*: *Texte zu dem Streite zwischen Glauben und Wissen im Islam* (Bonn, 1913).

Hourani: *Ibn Rushd (Averroes)*: *Kitāb faṣl al-maqāl*, ed. G. F. Hourani (Leiden: E. J. Brill, 1959).

Ibn al-Abbār, *Takmila*: *Kitāb at-takmila li kitāb aṣ-ṣila*, ed. F. Codera in *Bibliotheca Arabico-Hispana*, V-VI (Madrid, 1887-89).

Ibn Abī Uṣaybi'a, *'Uyūn al-anbā'*: *'Uyūn al-anbā' fī ṭabaqāt al-aṭibbā'*, ed. A. Müller (Königsberg, 1884), 2 vols.

Ibn Bājja, *Tadbīr*: *Kitāb tadbīr al-mutawaḥḥid*, ed. and Span. tr. M. Asín Palacios, *El regimen dei solitario por Avempace* (Madrid-Granada, 1946).

Ibn Ḥazm, *Fiṣal*: *Kitāb al-fiṣal fil-milal*, Span. tr. M. Asín Palacios, *Abenházam*.

Ibn Khaldūn, *Histoire des Berbères*: *Kitāb al-'ibar*, in *Histoire des Berbères*, Fr. tr. M. de Slane, 2nd ed. P. Casanova (Paris, 1927), 3 vols.

Muqaddima: in *Prolégomènes d'Ebn Khaldoun*, ed. E. M. Quatremère (Paris, 1858), 3 vols.

Ibn Khallikān, *Wafayāt: Kitāb wafayāt al-a'yān wa anbā' abnā' az-zamān* (Cairo, 1859). Eng. tr. M. de Slane (Paris, 1842-71), 4 vols.

(Ibn Rushd), **Kitāb bidāyat al-mujtahid wa nihāyat al-muqtaṣid fil-fiqh* (Cairo, 1952).

Comm. on Pl. Rep.: Averroes' commentary on Plato's 'Republic', Heb. ed. and Eng. tr. E. I. J. Rosenthal (Cambridge, 1956).

Ḍamīma: Appendix to *Faṣl*, in Hourani (text), with references to pages and lines in Mr.

Faṣl: Kitāb faṣl al-maqāl wa taqrīr mā bayn ash-sharī'a wal-ḥikma min al-ittiṣāl, in Hourani (text), with references to pages and lines in Mr.

Manāhij: Kitāb al-kashf 'an manāhij al-adilla fī 'aqā'id al-milla, wa ta'rīf mā waqa'a fīhā bi-ḥasb at-ta'wīl min ash-shibah al-muzīgha wal-bida' al-muḍilla, in Mr. Mr. pp. 122-27 in Hourani.

Summary of Aristotle, De physico auscultu, in *Rasā'il Ibn Rushd* (Hyderabad, 1947).

Summary of Aristotle, Metaph., in *Rasā'il Ibn Rushd* (Hyderabad, 1947). Germ. tr. S. Van den Bergh, *Die Epitome der Metaphysik des Averroes* (Leiden, 1924).

Tafsīr: Tafsīr mā ba'd aṭ-ṭabī'a, ed. M. Bouyges (Beirut, 1938-51), 4 vols. (The *Great commentary* on Aristotle's *Metaphysics*).

Tahāfut: Tahāfut at-tahāfut, ed. M. Bouyges (Beirut, 1930). Eng. tr. S. Van den Bergh, *Averroes' Tahafut al-tahafut* (London, 1954), 2 vols.

Ibn Sīnā, *Ishārāt: Kitāb al-ishārāt wat-tanbīhāt*, ed. J. Forget (Leiden, 1892).

Najāt: Kitāb an-najāt, ed. M. S. Kurdī (Cairo, 1938).

Ibn Ṭufayl, *Ḥayy*: *Ḥayy Ibn Yaqẓān*, ed. and Fr. tr. L. Gauthier, *Hayy Ben Yaqdhân, roman philosophique d'Ibn Thofaïl* (Beirut, 1936).

Jawāhir: Al-jawāhir al-ghawālī min rasā'il al-imām ḥujjat al-Islām al-Ghazālī, ed. M. S. Kurdī (Cairo, 1934).

K.: *Kitāb*.

Kindī, *Kitāb al-Kindī ilal-Mu'taṣim*, ed. A. F. Ahwānī (Cairo, 1948).

Lane: Lane, E. W., *Arabic-English lexicon* (London, 1863-92), 8 vols.

* In references to works of Ibn Rushd I do not mention the author's name.

Marrākushī, *Mu'jib:* 'Abd al-Wāḥid al-Marrākushī, *Kitāb al-mu'jib fī talkhīṣ akhbār al-Maghrib*, 2nd ed. R. Dozy (Leiden, 1885).

Mr.: Müller, M. J., *Philosophie und Theologie von Averroes* (Munich, 1859). (*Faṣl, Manāhij, Ḍamīma*, Ar. ed.)

Mr. tr.: Müller, M. J., *Philosophie und Theologie von Averroes* (Munich, 1875). (German tr. of above.)

Pl. *Rep.*: Plato, *Republic.*

Qur'ān: Al-Qur'ān al-karīm, Azhar ed. (Cairo, 1918).

Renan, E., *Averroès: Averroès et l'Averroïsme*, 3rd ed. (Paris, 1866).

Schacht, J., *Origins: The origins of Muhammadan jurisprudence* (Oxford, 1950).

Strauss, L., *Persecution: Persecution and the art of writing* (Glencoe, Illinois, 1952).

Wensinck, *Concordance:* Wensinck, A. J., *Concordance de la tradition musulmane* (Leiden, 1936-42), 2 vols.

INDEX TO THE TRANSLATION

Numbers refer to the pages of Müller's edition, printed in the margins of the translation. (*Decisive treatise:* 1-26. *Appendix:* 128-31. *Extract:* 122-27.) The summaries inserted in the translation are not indexed.

Entries for abstract nouns, e.g. "belief", include references to related English forms, e.g. "believe", "believers", except in a few cases of separate listing.

Arabic originals of English words are placed in parentheses. Cross references are given where the same Arabic word is translated by two or more English words.

Printed and bound by CPI Group (UK) Ltd, Croydon, CR0 4YY
18/03/2025
01834104-0001